HOME OWNERSHIP IN THE INNER CIT

Frontispiece   Enveloping in Birmingham

    A.   In progress, Phillimore Road, Saltley

    B.   Completed, George Arthur Road, Saltley

Home Ownership in the Inner City

Salvation or Despair?

VALERIE KARN
Professor of Environmental Health and Housing
University of Salford
JIM KEMENY
National Swedish Institute for Building Research
PETER WILLIAMS
Assistant Director, Institute of Housing

Gower

Published by

Gower Publishing Company Limited,
Gower House,
Croft Road,
Aldershot,
Hants GU11 3HR,
England

Gower Publishing Company,
Old Post Road,
Brookfield,
Vermont 05036
U.S.A.

British Library Cataloguing in Publication Data

Karn, Valerie A.
  Home ownership in the inner city : salvation or
  despair?——(Studies in urban and regional policy).
  1. Home ownership——Social aspects——England
  2. Cities and towns——England
  I. Title   II. Kemeny, J.   III. Williams, Peter
  1946 July 13-   IV. Series
  333.3'23   HD7287.82.G7

Library of Congress Cataloging-in-Publication Data

Karn, Valerie Ann.
  Home ownership in the inner city.

  (Studies in urban and regional policy ; 3)
  Bibliography: p.
  Includes index.
  1. Home ownership--England--Birmingham--Case
studies. 2. Home ownership--England--Liverpool--Case
studies. I. Kemeny, Jim. II. Williams, Peter,
1947-   . III. Title. IV. Series.
HD7287.82.G72B575 1986   333.33'8   85-17608

ISBN 0-566-05056-0

Printed in Great Britain by Paradigm Print, Gateshead, Tyne & Wear.

Contents

Plates and maps

Tables

Page

Acknowledgements

The authors are very grateful to the many people who have helped us with this research, in particular the people who gave their time to answering the questionnaires. We would like, however, to single out for thanks at least some of those who were especially closely involved in the research. These are Ray Boot of the Inner Cities Directorate for his role as our co-ordinator in the Department of the Environment; Joy Marcuse and Ian Marcuse for their work in organising data collection and preparation; Chris Raine and Peter Cook and other officers of the Liverpool City Planning Department for their assistance in selecting the Liverpool Survey area and for subsequent comments on the draft report; Terry Brunt and Trevor Edwards of Birmingham City for help and advice on the City's urban renewal and housing programmes; Geoff Green, Alan O'Dell, Jeff Henderson, Roland Watkins and John McQuillan and staff at the Building Research Establishment for their help with the maintenance and condition surveys; Jean Trainor, Bruce Stafford, Larry Cromwell and Suzanne Sheridan for providing research assistance, and our secretaries Florence Denton and Joan Morgan. We would also like to express particular gratitude to all those officers in the Inner Cities and Housing Directorates of the Development of Environment who gave help and encouragement with the revisions of the draft. Finally, we are grateful to the City Planning Department at Liverpool and the Urban Renewal Department in Birmingham for permission to publish their photographs, and to Sheila Milne for compiling the index.

Though this research was funded by the Inner Cities Directorate of the Department of Environment, its conclusions are those of the authors alone and do not necessarily represent the views of the Department of Environment.

STUDIES IN URBAN AND REGIONAL POLICY

Series Editor: Andrew Thomas

This book is one of a series on Urban
and Regional Policy published by Gower in
Association with the Centre for Urban and
Regional Studies. The series is intended to
provide a vehicle for findings in the broad
field of urban and regional studies with a
particular emphasis on the dissemination of
empirical and theoretical research.

Studies in Urban and Regional Policy
complements the existing range of Centre
publications. These are designed to find a
wide audience for the results of continuing
research in the fields of housing, regional
and local economic development, planning and
leisure and tourism. These areas of interest
have been developed through funding from
central and local government, research
councils and charitable trusts since the
Centre was established in 1966 as a
Department of the Faculty of Commerce and
Social Science at the University of
Birmingham.

1 Introduction

INTRODUCTION

In the nearly forty years since the end of the Second World War,
Britain has passed through several phases of development and change.
The early post-war consensus allowed a whole series of important social
and economic reforms to be instituted through the state, giving much
support to those who have argued for a new brand of state capitalism.
The terminology of planning and control became commonplace as the
technocrats sought to replace the market in many spheres of social
life. These reforms were carried comfortably into subsequent decades
by the post-war boom. In the 1950s and 1960s both society and the
built environment underwent processes of renewal. The slogan 'You've
never had it so good' had considerable reality, though the grinding
poverty experienced by many remained, temporarily obscured by general
levels of affluence. Cities and urban areas in general were expanding
in size as their centres were rebuilt and their suburbs sprawled.
Urban problems were identified as being related to growth, traffic and
an outworn environment. The solutions were those of the new era:
central redevelopment, high rise housing, new roads and decentralisation.

Only in the late 1960s and early 1970s as Britain's economic
situation began to worsen sharply, did many of the post-war shibboleths
begin to fall. The financial costs of intervention in the market were
recognizably large and a cause of growing concern. Moreover, with
respect to the built environment those costs were large in both
financial and social terms. The residents of inner city areas (as they
were now seen - in contrast to outer suburbia) resented the
paternalistic and often brutal approach of government authorities in
carrying out redevelopment plans. As the experience of the process
grew so resistance hardened. This pressure, along with financial
stringency and growing doubts about the success of high rise housing,
resulted in a move, which gathered momentum throughout the 1970s, away
from comprehensive redevelopment to renewal programmes which combined
small scale redevelopment with large scale campaigns to refurbish
existing stock (Paris and Blackaby, 1979; Dunleavy, 1981; Gibson and
Langstaff, 1982). This process was paralleled by other important
shifts. In many urban areas the inner-most districts had long been
dominated by private landlords (though not everywhere - in some cities
and towns, inner city home ownership levels have always been high).
Their holdings had been frozen by rent control and then, with the
uncertainty surrounding redevelopment, their market value had been
substantially undermined. By the late 1960s it was clear to most
landlords that neither a Conservative nor a Labour government was
likely to reinvigorate the private rental sector, despite all the

rhetoric that flowed. Sales to would-be home owners provided one possible outlet. The question was who would buy?

Inner city home ownership

To answer this question properly would require a detailed account of the development of British society in the post-war era as well as a comprehensive study of the labour and housing markets. A brief summary must suffice.

The substantial number of West Indians and Asians who moved to Britain in the decades following World War II form one important group of purchasers of inner city housing. Disadvantaged in the labour market, in the bureaucratically managed public housing system and in the private rental market, many of these households 'opted' to buy cheap inner city dwellings. Their own community networks were sufficient to allow them to raise informal loans to circumvent the institutional barriers to home ownership which had been erected by the housing finance agencies - most notably by the building societies.

A second group of purchasers was drawn from the existing residents of inner areas and their children. Despite the problems of credit many households opted to buy their dwellings, reflecting amongst other things the growing recognition that ownership was both possible and desirable. Some obtained mortgages from local authorities or used rental purchase schemes or other arrangements with their landlord; others had short term high interest loans. Some came unstuck in the process but most, often sustained by having two or more earners in the household, were able to win through and complete the purchase. Inflation in wages carried most individuals to a safe point in their purchase plans. A third group, rarely talked of outside London but actually present in most towns and cities, consisted of the gentrifying middle class. Gentrification has been described in dramatic ways which are rarely met in reality. Certainly the process of takeover and displacement can be a major cause of friction and distress, and the transformation of certain urban areas is startling. However, much of this middle class takeover occurs in a more mundane and less obvious way - academics, professionals and the like buying into working class areas and maintaining a low key lifestyle. This has happened throughout cities and, even in areas where people claim gentrification would never occur, one finds such households already in occupation.

To understand the behaviour of each of these three groups requires much analysis. The changing structure of the labour market, with the shift from blue collar to white collar work, the deskilling of traditional craft-based employment, and the growth of distribution and service-based activities have all contributed to the changes observable in these areas. Some 'client' groups have contracted while others have expanded and as always the built environment reflects and structures this process. The form and the function of the family has altered too, with women moving into the labour force in large numbers, creating two-earner households with enhanced purchasing power. Alongside, that has been a changing class structure with a rapid expansion of professional, managerial and white collar occupations which served to blur traditional class distinctions. Place of residence, as a crucial

reflection of one's place in the social system, has altered
accordingly.

Changes such as these, along with the new geography of production
(i.e. the development of outer suburban sites), new directions in state
intervention and an altered investment market in which residential,
commercial and industrial property, as well as shares, precious metals
and other commodities, have grown in importance, have resulted in
disinvestment by some groups in the inner city and investment by
others. Whether the former is compensated by the latter is one of the
questions we tackle in this book. However, the point we wish to
establish at this stage is that the context within and around the inner
city has changed dramatically over the last forty years (Forrest, et
al., 1980; Hebbert, 1981). Far from being stable, entrenched
communities insulated from change, the inner areas, like other parts of
the city, have been undergoing constant change.

The inner city

In the 19th century the areas adjacent to the economic core of the city
were viewed with considerable trepidation by the middle classes. These
were seen as the areas where revolutionary ideas were bred and where
mob violence ruled (Stedman-Jones, 1971). Alternatively, it was
disease, immorality, ill health and social decay that were seen to
emanate from these places threatening to contaminate the rest of
society, just as the ideas that bred there could destroy the social
structure. As Hebbert (ibid.) and others argue, 'the inner city' was a
mixed metaphor for a whole range of concerns. The clearances
undertaken by local authorities, the intervention of two world wars and
a depression, and the establishment of a limited but important set of
land use and public health regulations ensured that these inner areas,
while still highly problematic in terms of what to do with them, were
not perceived as potential threats to society in the early twentieth
century. They were recognised as centres of poverty though poverty was
just as apparent in many rural areas. They were also a focus of
government attempts to intervene - most notably, via the reduction of
population in the 'crowded districts' and the provision of suburban
public housing.

By the end of the 1950s it was apparent that concern was mounting
once again regarding the inner areas. In the main this was because
race had now made a renewed and forceful entry into the British social
landscape and into British national politics. In London, 'race riots'
had taken place and in a few major cities 'immigrant' residential areas
were emerging, more in reputation than reality but still sufficient to
sway the concerns of the more sensitive politicians. During the 1960s
and 1970s these concerns slowly built into a veritable 'race industry'.
It was also during the 1960s that the continuance of widespread poverty
was acknowledged. The question then posed was how to explain this
amidst general affluence. A series of area based research/action
projects, major inquiries and new policies were put into operation
though much doubt has been expressed regarding their value or
effectiveness (e.g. Bridges, 1981/2). Race, poverty and deprivation
thus became firmly associated with the inner areas of Britain's cities
during the 1970s and increasingly talk was in terms of an 'inner city
crisis'.

It is in the context of these more general concerns that we have undertaken this specific piece of research on inner city home ownership. In 19 the government announced a new inner city policy, setting up partnerships with local governments and county councils and funding a new programme of research. This study is part of that programme. While our work has clearly been informed and influenced by both research and opinion regarding the nature of the inner city and the problems it contains, it is also important, however, that we locate this study with respect to the rise of home ownership and the problems and prospects for that tenure in the 1980s. It is to this we now turn.

Home ownership

The rise of home ownership has been one of the most salient features of post-war Britain. In 1945, approximately 25 per cent of households owned or were buying their own homes. By 1981 this had risen to 56 per cent and by 1984 to over 60 per cent. Aside from the overall trend, it is apparent that ownership is now widespread among groups who had largely been excluded from this tenure in the pre-war era. Thus large numbers of skilled and semi-skilled workers (and to a lesser extent unskilled workers) are now home owners. This expansion has come about partly through rising affluence and government assistance and partly through declining or restricted rental opportunities. Whatever the cause, the transformation in tenure arrangements - from a dominance of renting to a dominance of owning - is seen by many to be one of the great successes of post-war Britain. Its growth has been accompanied by rising consumption of a whole range of durable goods, such as cars, washing machines and televisions and an array of services related to leisure and communications. The consequences of all these changes are that home ownership is now the dominant tenure and considerable political importance is attached to its growth and maintenance (see Merrett, 1982 for a useful discussion of the rise of ownership).

The expansion of home ownership has inevitably exposed many of the weaknesses associated with this tenure: for example, the problems of maintaining mortgage payments in times of rising unemployment; the tendencies to under-invest in structural maintenance and for some owners to tolerate very low standards, mainly as a consequence of low incomes; the difficulties brought about by fluctuations in the supply and cost of mortgage finance; the caution of financial institutions especially with respect to moving the tenure downmarket, that is, to successively cheaper dwellings and/or lower income households; the costs and vagaries of the buying and selling process and the role of market intermediaries such as estate agents, brokers and dealers; the problems of area differences in supply and demand with consequential impact upon the mobility of owners; and, finally, the costs to the state of ever-increasing levels of assistance in order to sustain and maintain the home-ownership sector.

Many of these difficulties have been foreshadowed over the years (Bowmaker, 1895, Cole 1943) although it is apparent that little serious analysis of the home ownership sector has been undertaken. Typically the view has existed that once a person obtained a public tenancy or became a home-owner their housing problems were over. As we are now well aware, that simply is not so and home ownership, like public housing has major weaknesses as well as major strengths. In part this is because housing stands at the intersection of so many relationships. As we argued earlier in this introduction, the links between the job market and housing are strong and both are necessities. The wage influences what housing can be obtained while housing costs and location influence labour supply and labour costs. Similarly housing costs, conditions and locations intersect with questions related to access to shops, services, education and to matters of health, family life and social advancement. Housing is a vital matter in the life of any nation and as a consequence it is high on the political agenda.

If the housing question as a whole is at a juncture of many relationships, then this is doubly true with respect to housing in the inner city. As indicated earlier, 'the inner city' is a term which has become a shorthand for a whole array of social tensions since the 1960s. Vandalism, crime, poverty, unemployment, racial tensions, decay, destitution, prostitution, worn-out environment, poor housing and schools, drunks and drug addicts - all these and more run together into a collage of images which collectively are viewed as being 'the inner city problem'. In addressing questions related to inner city home ownership, we are inevitably drawn into this vortex of social concern. Given the many dangers of researching such a complex and highly publicised arena, it is important that we spell out our view of the issues to be addressed with respect to home ownership in the inner city.

We have deliberately sought to develop a sense of the social context within which we are working. We will now specify, as briefly as possible, both the issues we have addressed through our research and the conceptual stance we have adopted in undertaking this work. We also have to add that many of our findings are damaging to the image of home ownership and that as a consequence we have met obstacles to their publication. We believe, however, that it is essential that such information should be readily available not simply as a critique of this tenure but also as a basis for reforms. Throughout our aim is to offer critical but ultimately constructive assessment of the issues at hand.

The issues

There is a great danger when tackling as complex an issue as the role of inner city home ownership that one may be absorbed into a series of very detailed concerns and fail to see the general context surrounding them and the broad trajectories into which they fit. Our aim here is both to consider the intricacies of the situation and also to make links to broader circumstances. So far in this introduction we have considered these issues at a most general level. We now turn to the many important detailed questions concerning inner city home ownership. The main issues can be usefully grouped under three headings: the housing market; housing finance; and government and housing policy.

The housing market

Perceptions of the inner city housing market vary widely depending upon the city involved. For London, the image is of gentrification even though many areas, noticeably in the East End, have been only partially affected by this. For Liverpool and Birmingham, it is a perception of redevelopment with residual owner-occupied and private rent sectors. Whatever the city concerned there is a widespread assumption that cheap property there provides the first rung on a home ownership ladder which reaches out to the suburbs. Moreover, there is an assumption that the market in these areas operates in similar ways to all other areas, experiencing similar support from government and financial institutions, similar price inflation and similar market functions for agents and brokers. The reality with respect to all these matters is that the inner city market has many distinct features reflecting the concentrations of types of people and property in these areas.

In recent years a considerable amount of research has been conducted on the question of 'redlining' (e.g. Weir, 1976, Stevens et al., 1982, Williams, 1978). As this indicates, inner city owners have to confront a very complex institutional structure when trying to buy or sell. Overall the precise form of the market is less well known and as we show later, very few of the expectations outlined above are met which suggests that the whole matter of low income inner city ownership is highly problematic. The performance of the market in these areas in terms of price movement is much less 'impressive' than elsewhere. This leads us to suggest that, far from providing a ladder up the housing market, buying a house in these areas could ultimately constitute a major trap.

This concern is reinforced when one considers housing quality. Recent house condition surveys have indicated the growing levels of disrepair in the owner-occupied stock (Department of Environment, 1983). Since this disrepair has not yet provoked a major rupture in the market, that is, housing being abandoned as too poor, it has not been treated as a matter of paramount concern. However, the concentrations of undermaintained property in inner areas force a rethink on this matter. The combination of poor houses and poor people, who are unable to maintain their homes even in their current condition, suggests that a downward spiral must now be in operation. Renewal, albeit with the aid of government grants, begins to look very problematic. In Birmingham the levels of aid have been enhanced substantially through the adoption of the 'enveloping'(1) scheme and smaller initiatives such as the purchase and improve scheme but even this expanded programme begins to look inadequate when set against the scale of the problem and has in any case subsequently fallen victim to expenditure cuts.

Housing has been seen by many as one of the key components of the inner city question. As our research will show, considerable doubt must be cast on the assumption that a rising level of home ownership marks an important and progressive transformation of the situation by replacing private landlords who do not invest with home owners who do. Indeed, because the market is now in the hands of many individuals rather than a smaller number of landlords or of local government, disinvestment may in total be proceeding at a faster pace, especially in the light of unemployment and continuing low incomes in these areas.

These problems take on a further dimension when we reintroduce the question of race. For the variety of reasons outlined earlier the inner city housing market in Birmingham, as in a number of other cities, is dominated by West Indians and Asians. The downward spiral of house condition and house price is noticeable across the spectrum of property whether owned by black or white occupants. However, it is apparent that price in particular is falling fastest in Asian areas. Given the financial mechanisms adopted by many Asians and particularly their dependence on loans from the limited resources of the local community itself, the question of disinvestment and the inner city as a trap looms even larger, with enormous implications for race relations in Britain.

Housing finance

This leads directly into concerns with the finance market as a whole. Many mortgage lenders assume that where they do not lend, no market exists. Research has shown that to be totally incorrect (e.g. Karn, 1976). More importantly, however, for the last decade mortgage finance agencies, stung by criticism and responding to government persuasion and threats regarding the extension of ownership, have made much of their moves downmarket and their lending in areas where previously they were reluctant to tread. Building societies, for example, often point to the increased share of mortgages going to the purchase of pre-1919 houses. The research we have conducted enables us to follow in a precise manner the realities of these claims. Not surprisingly perhaps, they are found wanting. Lending patterns still show systematic bias, albeit that we qualify this by recognition of the variations between different lenders and between branches of the same lender. However, neither local government nor building societies, what might be termed the conventional lenders, can be seen as adequately serving the market with the result that buyers often have to resort to high-cost loans with restrictive provisions that are ineligible for government assistance via tax relief. The nature of the finance available and the relationships through which that market operates open up a whole range of complex questions regarding equitable and just treatment (Lansley and Goss, 1981). The informality of the system does, in part, lead to abuse just as in other respects it gives enormous flexibility.

Government and housing policy

Inevitably all of the issues we have briefly covered here involve government at one level or another. We have already discussed government concern with the inner city and, even though the extent of that commitment might be questioned, government is at least obliged to consider many of the issues raised and has in many cases implemented policies which were supposed to deal with them. The complexity of the position has unfortunately confounded many of the simpler approaches adopted. Having removed itself by withdrawing from comprehensive redevelopment, government now finds itself increasingly involved again via different mechanisms. The market in these areas has notable imperfections. The choices of consumers are highly constrained, a product less of the market they are operating within than of those beyond its borders. The financial situation with respect to the supply of mortgages is also confused. Incentives and encouragement to the private institutions that provide the funds, the banks and building societies, have only moderated the position. As yet government has avoided compulsion and is now confronted by the possibility of transgressing one or more of its principles. In other words the inner city market throws up major contradictions for consumers, suppliers and government. The Government's ambivalence towards the building societies is in part a reflection of the societies' capacity to obscure the issue. Their so called non-profit, non-market status enables them to hide behind a whole variety of guises through which government finds it difficult to break.

Government support for home ownership is unquestionable but its capacity to keep providing new resources is now in doubt. Detailed analysis of inner city home ownership reveals the problem that it has many of the qualities of 'a lame duck'. Certainly better co-ordination is possible and local government could act in a far more positive way than at present but all of this requires a commitment actually to specify and consider a range of complex and highly political issues. For the present at least we wonder whether that commitment exists. We would also ask whether the resources to prop up and modify the present situation will be made available given other pressures and priorities. Of course, that opens up the question of whether other approaches could be adopted. We believe they could and that in the long run they may well be cheaper. In other words, we question whether home ownership is the most appropriate solution for inner city residents or the inner city. The alternatives to individualised initiatives (however much individual initiatives are backed by the state) are new forms of joint ventures, co-operative housing and new styles of redevelopment and renewal by government. As the bill for maintaining the status quo gets bigger perhaps these will be considered more fully.

Even if government remains unshakeable in its commitment to home ownership, it could consider questions related to the operation of the market in these areas. It is clear from our study that considerable abuses exist many of which are potentially soluble given the appropriate climate. Again, it is necessary to concede that the market is not infallible and that problems arise which can be tackled without overturning every principle attached to its operations. Just as we can criticise statism, we should also be aware of the failings of the market.

OUR APPROACH

The politics of research

This research was commissioned by the Inner Cities Directorate of the Department of the Environment whose original expressed object was to publish the results as one of a series of monographs. To this end each research team was asked to produce a report of a standard length incorporating the empirical findings of the study. The project would not be deemed to be completed and financial arrangements settled until this report had been submitted. Permission to publish other articles or address seminars even after the final report was submitted was refused on the grounds that it would be inappropriate to disclose findings which had not received ministerial approval. (Standard Department of Environment research contracts give the Department the power to exercise such a veto within the period of the contract and for two years after the submission of the final report but in the past it had been a norm to give rather than withhold, permission). Our report was submitted in April 1982. It then went through numerous revisions to produce a draft that the civil servants were willing to submit to the relevant ministers, namely Mr. John Stanley and Mr. Tom King. At the end of this process, the civil servants expressed informally a willingness to recommend the draft for publication by the Department. Further delays ensued however and it was only after the Select Committee on Urban Renewal had requested it for evidence in December 1982 that the draft was finally shown to the ministers, but with only a neutral statement, not the promised recommendation to publish. (This probably made no difference since the Sheffield University's report on the inner city private rented market in Sheffield (Crook and Bryant, 1983) was recommended for publication but was also refused by the minister.)

In January 1983 we were informed that the Department would not publish but that we were to be allowed to do so ourselves. Repeated requests for a written statement giving the reasons for the refusal produced the following on 1st March 1983.

It was felt that there had been a number of recent developments in Government policy which for reasons which we duly appreciated, would not be reflected in your own work carried out somewhat earlier.

This statement seems curious considering the nine months of revisions during which no such reservations were expressed. More important it is our belief that the findings of our report are of the greatest relevance to policies such as the right to buy, shared ownership etc, incorporating as these policies do the belief that home ownership in itself solves the housing problems of lower income families.

Even though we have been given permission to publish, we are still hedged about with constraints. The draft report was written and revised with a view to publication by the Department of Environment, not a commercial publisher, but we are not allowed to make any further alterations to it without restarting a lengthy approval process. So that we do not lose many more months or risk outright refusal to let us publish at all, we have decided to publish the report as it stands but with this lengthy introduction to provide background to the study, even though, inevitably, there will be some disjuncture between this section and the body of the report. One of the revisions we had to agree to is not to name any of the financial institutions, other than the local authorities, we have found operating (or refusing to operate) in the areas we have studied. This restriction means that the section of Chapter 5 on variable lending practices between building societies and between their branches, loses much impact.

As will be apparent upon reading the text the study is basically empirical. Our original plan was to produce a number of empirical interim reports which presented the findings in detail, and to produce a conceptual and policy-oriented discussion document which would not be overburdened with statistics. Such a book would have enabled us to refer readers to the data in interim reports and to have concentrated upon the crucial research task of analysis and discussion. Because of the requirement to produce an empirical report as our final submission to the Department of Environment and because of the labour involved in preparing this for publication we have not yet had the opportunity to develop our theoretical treatment of inner city home ownership as much as we would have wished. It also means that much of the report has been written without explicit recourse to ongoing academic and policy debates about the questions under consideration. This is clearly a problem. Deprived of their social context most of these facts are prey to whatever interpretation can be laid upon them. Our aim in this introduction is to forestall the risk of misinterpretation by laying out briefly the framework which, implicitly at least, guided our research.

ORGANISATION OF THE BOOK

We have already described in general terms the contents of this book. Essentially the volume provides a detailed account of recent home purchase in several inner area neighbourhoods of Birmingham and Liverpool. The contents are organised to reflect the process of collecting and analysing the data we assembled to assess this situation. In the introduction we discuss the general focus of the study and draw the links between this work and a previous project undertaken by one of the authors (Karn, 1976). We also describe the surveys which were undertaken. The subsequent chapters report on specific aspects of these surveys, i.e. in Chapter 2 we discuss house prices and finance, in Chapter 3 the search for housing and in Chapter 4 the search for a loan. The implications of the way in which the housing market operates are expressed in our discussion of housing conditions (Chapter 5) and analysed in policy terms in the concluding chapter. We make no apology for this straightforward organisation. We adopted the view that by keeping the structure simple we were most likely to complete the work and to provide the basic information we were required to supply. It is our intention to develop the account presented here into a much fuller analysis of the inner city.

INTERPRETATION

Within geography, politics, economics, sociology and history there has been an enormous upsurge of interest in recent years in the form and functioning of urban areas. Questions of land ownership, social movements, industrial restructuring, access and equity, class relations and interest-group politics have been amongst the many topics addressed. The work has sought not only to address issues related to the future of cities but also to understand the historical trajectories along which they may be proceeding. In developing such arguments and analysis it was perhaps inevitable that different modes of explanation should be propounded and this has resulted in a theoretical renaissance in the field of urban studies. There is not room here to discuss the many approaches. Fortunately, valuable summaries already exist, e.g. Bassett and Short, 1980a; Dunleavy, 1980; Elliot and McCrone, 1982; and Saunders, 1981. To classify them crudely, analysts have advanced Marxist, Weberian, neo-classical economic, psychological and simple empiricist theories of the city and the relations which are extant therein. Such a list is by no means exhaustive but it would not be unfair to suggest that the Marxist inspired urban political economy, developed most notably by Harvey, Lojkine and Mingione amongst others, has been of particular importance. Recently we can observe a number of attempts to develop an alternative position based around the work of Weber (e.g. Simmie, 1981; Saunders, 1981; Elliot and McCrone, 1982) drawing the analysis away from structural forces to questions of power and politics.

Our work has been substantially influenced by these debates (indeed, individually we have sought to contribute to them, e.g. Kemeny, 1982; Williams, 1982). We are firmly of the view that the housing market, especially in inner areas, is characterised by conflict rather than consensus and that the debate about choice versus constraint is a meaningless one (Karn, 1983a). We would also locate micro-level processes as part and parcel of a much broader set of forces. Thus, for us, questions of race and class tension in our study have to be understood within the context of British society as a whole, just as low income and unemployment in the inner areas are only explicable as part of the process of economic change and the structure of the economy. State intervention, which in our study areas takes a myriad forms, cannot simply be seen as progressive or benevolent; in many respects it acts to exacerbate and deepen the problems we observe.

In essence, we view the changes that are taking place in the inner cities of Birmingham and Liverpool as part of a process of residualisation. Increasingly throughout British society we can observe groups of people and physical areas that are being written out of the mainstream of societal development. As the requirements of production and the current economic environment change, they are outstripping the capacity of parts of the existing built environment to respond. As a consequence we now have 'redundant places and spaces' (to utilise part of the title of a book edited by Anderson, Duncan and Hudson, 1983). The same can be said with respect to people. High unemployment, deskilling and rapidly changing demands of labour, all set within the context of national and international shifts in the production and distribution system, are resulting in the creation of a massive underclass excluded from work and a reasonable income.

Now it is quite plain that such a description cannot be applied in any simple way to the areas we have studied or to other similar areas in Birmingham, Liverpool and elsewhere. In some respects 'normal life' has continued. However, we would argue that we can see the signs of a progressive downward shift in the prospects of both occupants and areas. They are being left behind even though on the surface they may appear to be conforming to the still widely held stereotype of the fortunate owner-occupier. The reality of their situation is however, grim. The properties are often unsound, housing costs high, and prospects poor. While we can identify opportunities to make the market more effective in these areas, we cannot ignore the broader changes which are taking place and which now and in the future will impact upon these people and these areas. It can be argued that the state is acting to prevent the residualisation process we have briefly outlined. Certainly, considerable funds have been made available and used but in reality they are a small proportion of what is needed and in no sense has any fundamental redistribution taken place. These areas are at best 'on hold'. It must be remembered that change is relative as well as absolute. We can point to many improvements in opportunities and conditions related to the inner city. But in doing so, we should not forget what has happened elsewhere. The rapid rise in executive incomes in comparison with those of manual workers is indicative of the gaps opening between different strata of society, as is the growing tendency of employers to pay wages below the legal minima (Guardian 2/1/84). Evidence from the relative movement of house prices also gives us clues about widening differentials in wealth.

We have indicated our belief, based upon long examination and analysis, that the situation for the inner city, and specifically for inner city home ownership is grim. We take this view, not as the product of some pre-ordained and theorised set of arguments but as a consequence of empirical work set within several streams of thought related to the inner city. It is impossible to deny the importance of structural change and we can see that this stands as an important explanatory factor for our study. However, such an argument carries with it a degree of fatalism and 'economism' with which we cannot agree. The social world, whether it be Britain, Birmingham or Saltley, is not produced without human action and however daunting 'macro' forces may be they are not immutable. Thus, while we agree with arguments that relate inner city decline to the functioning of the economy as a whole, we would stress a number of qualifications. All inner city areas are not the same. Each has its own history, present form and future in the same way that cities themselves vary in terms of their past, present and future status. These variations are important and should not be overlooked when erecting policies. In our areas, for example, we can contrast the frequency with which leasehold arises in Birmingham and its general absence in Anfield, Liverpool. Similarly there are important variations with respect to race and the relative position of each survey area in the housing market. The 'social ladder' in each city is complex and changing, with the consequence that one often fails to compare like with like. There seems to be a real difference in the role played by Anfield in Liverpool in contrast to Saltley in Birmingham. Each reflects the different contexts provided by the cities and regions concerned. The local political and administrative histories of the two cities are different and these flow through into local class and interest group mobilisation. We could go on - variations are enormous and complex ranging from different building types and financial and professional networks to employment, tradition and culture. Instead of one inner city problem, we have many, to the extent that rather than adopting that label - the inner city - we simply have sets of problems and relationships which combine differently area by area. As a rush of books and reports indicates (e.g. Hall, 1981), many problems are not unique to the inner city. They are widespread and commonplace in rural as well as urban areas. What is unique is the coalescence of forces social, political and economic which have made the inner city question into the problem. As argued earlier we believe race to have been an important explanation for this widespread social concern; the summer of riots in 1981 showed, however, how naive such concern is when it concentrates solely on racial deprivation and ignores class deprivation.

In presenting the findings of our study, we believe it essential that the work be linked to the kinds of arguments and issues outlined in this introduction. We hope that the empirical detail we provide can stand as a valuable supplement and support to the arguments being developed with respect to the inner city, and more generally regarding British society in the late 20th century. Unless there is a dramatic increase in levels of state intervention as well as changes in its relationships with market institutions such as financiers, agents and the building industry, it is difficult to see that the situation can do anything but worsen.

THE RESEARCH STUDY

As we indicated at the outset, this book is based upon a detailed study of inner city home ownership undertaken over the period 1979-1982. This research had three main aims: (1) to document the current financial arrangements for house purchase and the costs of owner occupation in a number of inner city areas in Birmingham and Liverpool; (2) to examine the way in which both the funding arrangements and the costs have changed in the eight years between 1972 and 1979 in the inner areas of Birmingham; (3) to consider the impact of those factors upon house improvement and maintenance and hence upon renewal policies for the inner city.

We were aware from the start that the term 'inner city' covered a wide variety of geographical, economic and social phenomena and that what we would study as 'inner city home-ownership' would be a product of our selection of study areas. Our research method made it inappropriate that we should select very scattered samples from many cities and our budget prevented us selecting more than a few study areas. We therefore freely acknowledge that ours is 'a study of owner-occupation in four areas of Birmingham and one in Liverpool', but, as we argue, our findings have a much wider applicability than just to these two cities.

Most important probably was our decision to study inner city owner-occupation only outside London. This meant that we did not attempt to take up the issue of 'gentrification' with its attendant advantages for renewal of the stock and problems for poorer households. Inevitably, having excluded London, our study was bound to be one of <u>relatively low income home ownership</u>, rather than just <u>inner city</u> home ownership. At a time when the policy is to increase owner-occupation down the income scales, this means that our findings are of wider relevance than even the issue of 'inner city' housing policy. Nevertheless, the 'inner city' dimension remains important in the sense that there are area effects produced by the depressed state of parts of the inner city, by selective suburbanisation of white and better-off families and by the age of the stock. The conjunction of all these factors appears to give the processes and outcomes of house purchase in our study a distinctive 'inner city' character. But most of the features discussed in this report are, in essence or in embryo, the problems encountered by any lower-income buyer, in that they relate to the basic problem that, when access is by ability to pay, an inadequate income can only buy an inadequate house.

The maintenance and extension of home ownership as the dominant tenure in Britain has been a central feature of government housing

policy in the 1980s. The continuing decline of the private rented
sector, curbs on expenditure on council housing and the growth of
council house sales have all tended to shift the focus of attention
towards home ownership as a solution to many housing problems. There
has been a steady rise in the level of home ownership in the last two
decades and efforts to expand the tenure continue with savings grants,
guarantee schemes, support lending, right-to-buy legislation subsidised
build for sale and improve for sale schemes, shared ownership and a
range of subsidies via the taxation system. The growth of home
ownership nationally has been paralleled by a growth in owner
occupation of older dwellings in the inner areas of cities. In the
inner areas we studied the proportions in 1981 ranged from 50 per cent
in Saltley to 65 per cent in Sparkhill. In all the areas studied there
had been sharp increases in the ten years between 1971 and 1981,
ranging from 14 per cent in Handsworth to 32 per cent in Saltley.

The levels of owner-occupation in our study areas were much higher
than the average in the London and Salford inner city partnership
areas, slightly higher than the average in the inner city partnership
areas in Manchester, Liverpool, Gateshead and Newcastle-on-Tyne, and
comparable with the average in Birmingham (see Appendix Table 3, p.
140). However, all these partnership areas had particular wards with
levels of owner-occupation comparable, to or even higher than, those in
our survey areas. The lessons from our study are therefore applicable
to circumstances in many of the country's other inner city areas. In
addition, since all the inner city areas have been experiencing sharp
increases in levels of home ownership, our findings are likely to have
growing relevance. In general terms inner area owner occupation
outside the wealthier parts of London can be associated with 'marginal'
purchasers, with low income home owners and with housing in poor
condition, though clearly important exceptions exist, e.g. affluent
areas such as Edgbaston in inner Birmingham. Whatever one thinks about
the desirability of the growth of home ownership in general, and in
these inner areas in particular, it has become apparent that in all of
Britain's cities the success or failure of inner area housing policies
and particularly of urban renewal policies is closely and increasingly
tied up with the fortunes of the low income owner occupier.

In the course of a Social Science Research Council sponsored project
entitled 'The Operation of the Housing Market in Immigrant Areas', a
substantial amount of work related to low income owners and the
financing of owner occupation was carried out (Karn, 1976, 1977,
1977/78, 1979). In part the project reported on here sought to develop
and up date some of that work in order to take account of current
circumstances and to build upon the important findings of the research.
The previous study concentrated upon three areas of Birmingham:
Saltley, Soho and Sparkhill. The survey results showed that of the
owner-occupiers who bought houses in these three areas between January
1972 and December 1974, only 27 per cent had conventional mortgages
that is from a building society or insurance company (15 per cent) or
local authority (12 per cent). Twenty two per cent had no formal loan
at all. Nationally at that time 85 per cent of all buyers with formal
loans got them from building societies and a further 9 per cent from
local authorities. Of those buyers with formal loans in these three
inner areas, 19 per cent had building society loans and 15 per cent
local authority loans, a total of 34 per cent.

One striking feature of the results was the difference between the three areas, all served by the same local authority and the same building societies. Local authority lending varied from 10 per cent in Saltley to 26 per cent in Soho, and building society lending from 9 per cent in Saltley to 43 per cent in Sparkhill. It emerged that building society lending in Sparkhill was very much concentrated in the 'white' end of the area and in the slightly newer streets. Whatever the cause, it was already clear from this earlier research that the financing of inner city home ownership was actually significantly different from the national pattern and that it was particularly vulnerable to the changing economic circumstances faced by both purchasers and the institutions that serviced them.

In undertaking research on inner city home ownership we are thus inquiring into an area central to many current policy debates. This book presents a summary version of our research findings, along with consideration of their immediate policy implications. Inevitably, the treatment is not fully comprehensive. As already noted we have not attempted here a full discussion of existing literature: nor have we expounded the theoretical implications of our research.

THE SURVEYS

The Inner City Home-ownership Project was made up of a number of constituent surveys which complement one another. The project as a whole builds upon an earlier survey conducted by Valerie Karn in 1974/75 and funded by the Social Science Research Council. The households who had bought between 1972 and 1974 were surveyed in three areas of inner Birmingham, at a rate of 1 in 2 in two areas and 1 in 3 in the third (See Appendix I). The areas were chosen using the 1971 Census as a means of identifying areas containing households of different ethnic mixes. Saltley was chosen as an area with mainly British and Pakistani-born households; Soho was chosen because it was expected to have a large proportion of West Indian-born households and Sparkhill was chosen as having mainly British-born households. (See Map 1).

The recent buyers surveys

A major element of the Inner City Home-ownership Project was to resurvey these areas in 1979/80 using the same sampling procedure but this time interviewing households who had bought between 1975 and 1979. In conjunction with the earlier survey this provided us with data covering buyers in all years between 1972 and 1979. In addition, because the resurvey covered five years instead of three, the numbers of interviews obtained were increased from around 100 per area to around 150 per area (for sampling methods and results see Appendix I).

Five inner city areas were surveyed in the course of the present project. Three of these were the areas surveyed in 1974. One additional area (Handsworth) was surveyed to attempt to locate an area of West Indian buyers, and an area of Liverpool (Anfield) was surveyed to obtain a sample of buyers from an inner city area where buyers born in Britain or Ireland predominated.

The Birmingham areas (see Map 1) covered a considerable proportion of the pre-1919 inner city housing stock in that city. In the three survey areas which had been covered in 1974 (Saltley, Soho and Sparkhill) and in Anfield, Liverpool (Map 2) the overwhelming majority of houses had been built before 1919. Handsworth differed from the other areas in that nearly half the stock had been built after 1919, mainly during the inter-war period, and this has proved most useful in placing the other areas in a broader urban context.

These surveys make up what are hereafter referred to as the recent buyers surveys'. In these, a considerable amount of data on various aspects of buying was collected on 622 households in Birmingham and 213 households in Liverpool. The interviewed households were drawn from those who had bought in each area between 1975 and 1979 and comprised samples of 1 in 2 of the total purchasers among private households in Sparkhill and Soho and 1 in 3 private households in Saltley, Handsworth and Anfield. Since in Birmingham the four survey areas cover a substantial proportion of the inner Birmingham area, the data provides a reliable picture of inner Birmingham buyers and their circumstances. In Liverpool, Anfield is typical of white, lower income areas of the inner city, but we did not have enough resources to cover ethnically mixed areas such as Liverpool 8. Our priority was to cover at least one predominantly white (2) area in an inner city. Together with the 1974 survey, the 1979 surveys also provide us with data in Birmingham covering most of the 1970s and so allow us to observe patterns of change over this period.

The house condition survey

Besides the recent buyers surveys, two additional surveys were carried out. The first was the condition survey. This was based on a one in five sub-sample from the recent buyers interviewed in 1979 in the four inner Birmingham areas. The condition survey, carried out by a qualified Public Health officer, obtained additional data on the state of repair and structural condition of the dwellings. The schedule was designed to be comparable with that of the English House Condition Surveys of 1976 and 1981. The survey was conducted in 1981 on a total of 130 dwellings. In addition, small numbers of households in this sub-sample were interviewed to obtain further information on their activities, attitudes and worries concerning repairs and maintenance.

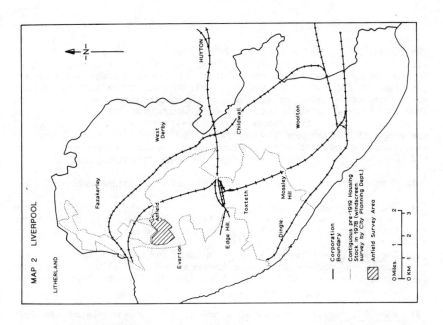

MAP 2   LIVERPOOL

——— Corporation Boundary

·········· Contiguous pre-1919 Housing Stock in 1978 (windscreen survey by City Planning Dept.)

▨ Anfield Survey Area

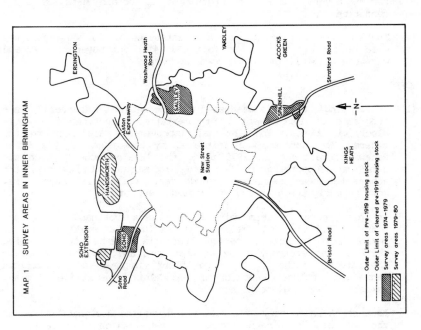

MAP 1   SURVEY AREAS IN INNER BIRMINGHAM

——— Outer Limit of Pre-1919 housing stock

········· Outer Limit of cleared pre-1919 housing stock

▨ Survey areas 1974–1979

▨ Survey areas 1979–80

The re-interview survey

The second additional survey was an attempt to locate and re-interview all those households who had been interviewed in the 1974 Birmingham buyers survey and who were still living at the same address. This was designed to follow up on the circumstances of those who had bought during the early 1970s to examine how their circumstances had changed. It also provided us with information on which households had moved and which had stayed. This survey - the re-interview survey - broadened the scope of the project beyond the narrower issue of recent buyers by examining the circumstances of longer-established owner-occupiers who had been previously interviewed when they were recent buyers.

In summary, then, the component surveys of the project were:

(1) The 1974 recent buyers survey: a one in two, or one in three sample of households buying between 1972 and 1974 in the inner Birmingham areas of Saltley, Soho and Sparkhill.

(2) The 1979 recent buyers survey: a one in two, or one in three survey of households buying between 1975 and 1979 in the inner Birmingham areas of Saltley, Soho, Sparkhill and Handsworth and in the inner Liverpool area of Anfield.

(3) The 1981 conditions survey: a one in five sub-sample of the 1979 recent buyers survey in Birmingham to obtain data on house condition.

(4) The 1980 re-interview survey: A re-interview of all households who were originally interviewed in the 1974 recent buyers survey and who were still living at the same address.

NOTES

(1) 'Enveloping', which is discussed in more detail in Chapter 7, is a programme of improvement of the external structure of a whole block of houses. The internal improvements are left to the owners. The concept was initiated by Birmingham City's Urban Renewal Department in 1979 using the 'Healey money' which was aimed at supporting the building industry. Subsequently, the scheme has been continued through various financial mechanisms, most recently the granting of Exchequer subsidies.

(2) In this report the term white is used as a shorthand for persons born in Britain and Ireland. It excludes a small number of persons born in Europe, America, Australia who might be considered white in the everyday sense of that word and who are classed in the category 'other'. The term 'black' is used in the American sense and includes West Indian and Asian buyers (i.e. Indian, Pakistani and Bangladeshi households).

As a check on country of birth, which was the designation used in the analysis, respondents were also asked which of a series of listed groups they felt they belonged to. There was a very close correspondence between country of birth and self-designated group.

2 Inner city buyers and their homes

We said in our introduction that we were aware that our study is not of all inner city areas, but just of four inner Birmingham areas and one in Liverpool. We said that the choice of areas, in particular our exclusion of London, had particular implications for the type of inner city home ownership we were looking at. In other words we chose areas of relatively low income home ownership. In addition, as the last chapter has shown, the original Birmingham areas were chosen to achieve ethnic diversity and Anfield was added to the 1979 study to obtain an area of white buyers which did not exist in Birmingham's inner city.

Given these features of our study, it is important for us to show first who the buyers were before going on to consider what sort of properties they were buying. For Saltley, Soho and Sparkhill we are able to compare features of the buyers in the 1972-74 period with those of buyers in 1975-79. For Anfield and Handsworth we have to be content with the 1975-79 results.

THE BUYERS

One of the main findings of the 1974 recent buyers survey in Soho, Saltley and Sparkhill was the very large percentage of Indian and Pakistani buyers. By the late 1970s this pattern had intensified (Table 2.1). Thus, in Saltley between 1972 and 1974, 69 per cent of buyers were Pakistani in origin but by 1975/79 this had risen to 73 per cent. In Soho the trend was even more marked. In 1972/74 69 per cent of buyers were of Asian origin (mainly Indian) and by 1975/79 this had risen to 82 per cent including East African Asians. In Sparkhill, the area with the lowest percentage of Asian buyers in 1972/74, the percentage had risen from 44 per cent to 58 per cent in 1975/79. It was particularly notable that the ethnic groups which were already predominant as buyers in each area in 1972/4 were even more so in 1975/79. The areas therefore appear to be becoming more homogeneous during this period in terms of the buying population. Sparkhill was the area of the three original survey areas which retained the greatest ethnic heterogeneity in its buyers. Handsworth was, however, similar to Sparkhill in its relative heterogeneity of buyers although, unlike Sparkhill, it contained a sizeable minority of West Indian buyers, 20 per cent in the 1975-79 period, as compared with 7 per cent in Soho, the only other inner city area where West Indians were buying in any numbers.

The decline in white buyers was most marked in Soho, where in the later period only 8 per cent of buyers were British or Irish, of whom nearly two-thirds were sitting tenant buyers. So active purchasing by

Table 2.1
Country of Birth of Head of Household (1972-1974 and 1975-1979 Buyers Survey)

	Inner Birmingham								Liverpool
Country of birth of head of household	Saltley		Soho		Sparkhill		Hands-worth	All 4 B'ham Areas	Anfield
	1972-1974	1975-1979	1972-1974	1975-1979	1972-1974	1975-1979	1975-1979	1975-1979	1975-1979
	%	%	%	%	%	%	%	%	%
England Scotland or Wales	19	18	12	7	37	25	24	18	98
Eire or Ulster	4	3	2	1	16	13	3	5	
Pakistan or Bangladesh	69	73	5	9	18	27	12	34	-
India	4	3	64	68	19	17	28	26	1
West Indies	2	2	14	7	2	3	20	8	-
East Africa	-	-	-	5	7	14	7	6	-
Other	3	1	4	4	3	1	6	3	1
Total	100	100	100	100	100	100	100	100	
N =	119	168	104	170	102	146	130	769*	213

* Weighted N.

Source: Surveys.

whites in that area was at a negligible level. Saltley, in comparison
had roughly sustained its level of white purchasers at 21 per cent
between 1975 and 1979 and only a seventh of these were sitting tenant
purchasers. Sparkhill's proportion of white buyers had fallen from 53
per cent in 1972-74 to 38 per cent in 1975-79, of whom just under a
third were sitting tenant purchasers. In Handsworth whites constituted
27 per cent of buyers between 1975 and 1979, of whom 5 per cent were
sitting tenants.

The ethnic composition of buyers in inner Birmingham and Anfield in
Liverpool differed markedly, as we intended in the choice of Anfield.
Thus, in the period 1975 to 1979, only 23 per cent of buyers in inner
Birmingham were British or Irish born, compared with no fewer than 98
per cent of Anfield buyers. However, in terms of socio-economic
status, white buyers in the two cities were very similar, although
buyers in Anfield and white buyers in Birmingham tended to have a
slightly higher status, with more non-manual and skilled manual
workers, than did Asian or West Indian buyers in inner Birmingham.
(Table 2.2). The Pakistani buyers were the least likely to have
non-manual or skilled manual occupations, followed by the Indians and
then by West Indians.

Incomes reflected these differences in socio-economic group. Buyers
in Anfield in 1980 (1) were slightly better off than those in
Birmingham in 1979 (Table 2.3). Over two-fifths (43 per cent) of
buyers there had net (head of household) incomes over £80 a week, as
compared with only 17 per cent in the four Birmingham areas.
Pakistanis had the lowest incomes, only 8 per cent over £80. The
highest incomes were amongst the British, Indians and West Indians (21
per cent over £80) and East Africans (17 per cent). The Anfield
buyers' incomes in 1980 were an average £5 higher than the net weekly
earnings of full-time employed males in Great Britain in 1979 (£70).
The Birmingham incomes in 1979 were £6 lower. Both, however, were far
below, indeed in a different category altogether, from the incomes
recorded for building society borrowers in that same year. There are
problems about making the comparison because of uncertainties about the
definition of the building society borrowers' incomes. The income is
that which was taken into account by the building society in assessing
the borrowers' ability to meet repayments. It may or may not include a
wife's earnings for instance. However, even taking this into account,
they were very much higher than any definition of income would produce
for the inner city buyers, because most of the latter were dependent
upon the single wage of a manual worker.

Family sizes were largest among Asians but among all ethnic groups
the overwhelming majority of households consisted of married couples
with or without children and with male heads of household in full-time
employment.

The previous tenure of British and Irish buyers in Birmingham was
also comparable with that of buyers in Anfield (see Table 2.4). Thus,
first-time buyers accounted for 84 per cent of British and Irish buyers
in Birmingham and of all buyers in Anfield as against only 65 per cent
of Pakistani and 69 per cent of Indian buyers in Birmingham. West
Indians occupied an intermediate position with 79 per cent being
first-time buyers. Averaged out, in Birmingham as a whole the

Table 2.2
Socio-economic Status of Buyers in Inner Birmingham and Liverpool
(1979 Buyers Survey)

Socio-economic status	Inner Birmingham		Anfield, Liverpool
	British and Irish buyers	Total	
	%	%	%
Professional and managerial	8	5	6
Clerical	14	8	15
Skilled manual	47	35	41
Semi-skilled manual	19	31	22
Unskilled manual	7	8	6
Other	5	13	11
Total %	100	100	100
N =	178 (weighted)	769 (weighted)	213

Source: Surveys.

Table 2.3
Head of Household Income (1979/80)

£.per week	Birmingham 4 Inner Areas 1979	Liverpool Anfield 1980	Great Britain Net weekly earnings for all jobs*, males in full-time employ-ment, 1979	Building Society Borrowers: incomes taken into account for mortgage 4th quart. 1979[+]		
					All buyers	1st-time buyers
	%	%	%		%	%
Up to 40	11	9	11			
41 - 50	9	10	13	Up to		
51 - 60	21	7	19	£77	9	10
61 - 70	23	13	17			
71 - 80	19	19	13			
81 - 90	8	15	15	£77-96	14	16
91 - 100	4	12				
101+	5	16	12	£96-115	17	17
				£115+	61	56
N =	734	183	6,145		715	391
Mean	£64	£75	£70		£130	£129

* Source : General Household Survey, 1979
+ Source : BSA Bulletin No. 22

Table 2.4
Previous Tenure of Buyers in Inner Birmingham and Liverpool
(1979 Buyers Survey)

	Inner Birmingham		Anfield, Liverpool
	British and Irish Buyers	Total	
	%	%	%
Owner-occupier	16	27	16
Council tenant	25	9	15
Housing association tenant	2	1	2
Private tenant	26	20	14
Lived with parents or no previous accom.	16	12	35
Lived with friends/ relatives	4	29	4
Other, including sitting tenants	12	3	14
Total %	100	100	100
N =	178 (weighted)	769 (weighted)	213

Source: Survey.

proportion of first-time buyers was 73 per cent. West Indian buyers and British and Irish buyers in both Birmingham and Anfield differed from the Asians in that a smaller percentage of the latter had been council tenants. The sitting tenant purchasers of private rented housing were almost invariably white. Very few white buyers had been sharing with friends or relatives, other than their parents, whereas the largest proportion of Asians had been with friends, or relatives (Table 2.5). In general, then, the British and Irish-born buyers in Anfield were very similar in their social characteristics to British and Irish born households who were buying in areas where, as an ethnic group, they were in a small minority.

The areas varied quite markedly in their tendency to attract buyers from outside the restricted area in and immediately around the survey area (Table 2.6). Anfield attracted people from the widest spread of areas: 54 per cent of buyers came from beyond the immediate vicinity of the survey area, 20 per cent of these from outside Liverpool. One factor in this was the return of council tenants from council estates outside Liverpool to the central city. Of the Birmingham areas, Handsworth most closely approached the Anfield model, with 37 per cent of buyers coming from beyond the surroundings of the survey area and only 24 per cent from the survey area itself. Sparkhill followed, still with only 25 per cent from the survey area, but with 52 per cent from its immediate surroundings. Soho had attracted very few outsiders at all, only 14 per cent from beyond the immediate surroundings of the survey area. Saltley presented a more mixed picture, recruiting a

Table 2.5
Previous Tenure by Country of Birth (Inner Birmingham weighted data)

Previous Tenure	England Scotland or Wales	Ulster or Eire	Pakistan or Bangladesh	India	West Indian	East Africa	Weighted total four areas
	%	%	%	%	%	%	%
Owner-occupier	12	(33)[+]	36	32	14	(12)	27
Council tenant	25	(23)	3	1	25	(2)	9
Housing assoc. tenant	2	(2)	–	–	10	–	1
Private tenant	24	(35)	7	14	34	(51)	20
Parents	20	(–)	5	20	3	(13)	12
Other relatives or friends	3	(7)	49	33	13	(23)	29
Other DK	15	(2)	–	1	–	–	3
Total	100	100	100	100	100	100	100
Weighted N=	142	36	263	210	77	45	769

[+] brackets are used when the total upon which the percentages are based is less than 50.
Source: Survey.

Table 2.6
Location of Previous Address of Buyers in Inner Birmingham and Anfield

Location of Previous Address	Birmingham Areas				Birmingham Weighted Total	Liverpool Anfield
	Saltley	Soho	Sparkhill	Handsworth		
	%	%	%	%	%	%
In survey area	58	46	24	23	40	21
Close to survey area	8	39	53	37	31	29
Elsewhere in Birmingham or West Mids. (Liverpool or Merseyside)	26	13	20	37	25	46
Elsewhere in Britain	7	2	3	4	4	4
Elsewhere	1	–	–	–	*	1
Total	100	100	100	100	100	100
N =	163	162	133	128	753	190

Source: Survey.

majority of its buyers (59 per cent) from the survey area itself but also attracting a third from areas outside the vicinity of Saltley. It had the largest proportion (8 per cent) arriving from outside the region. This pattern probably relates to three things. First, the very heavy predominance of Pakistanis in Saltley (see Table 2.1). Second, following from this, there is the attraction, for Pakistanis who move to Birmingham, of going to live in Saltley, and the ease with which arrangements can be made with fellow countrymen to help with the buying process. We will be returning to this issue later in the book (Chapters 4 and 5). Third, we are probably also seeing a loss of attraction of these areas for white buyers. As we already noted, white buyers are decreasing in numbers in all the Birmingham survey areas.

To summarise, Anfield and Handsworth appear to be attracting buyers from further afield than the other areas are. In fact a comparison with the 1972-4 buyers in Soho, Saltley and Sparkhill suggests that their attraction to outside buyers has been declining. The percentage of buyers who previously lived in the same survey area rose between the surveys, from 56 to 58 per cent for Saltley, from 35 to 46 per cent for Soho and from 11 to 24 per cent for Sparkhill. Wider geographical attraction also seems to be linked with numbers of first-time buyers. Saltley and Soho, the two areas with least outside buyers, had only 69 per cent and 67 per cent respectively of first-time buyers as compared with 79 per cent in Sparkhill, 77 per cent in Handsworth and 84 per cent in Anfield. The areas therefore appear to differ in the degree to which they function as a first step into home ownership for first-time buyers searching inner areas for properties they can afford. It is notable that among the four Birmingham areas this role is performed most clearly by Handsworth, which is at the top of the inner city market, and adjacent to the inter-war stock. This may partly be because most first-time buyers, as we have seen from building society statistics, have much higher incomes than the buyers surveyed in this study. But this cannot be the whole explanation because Anfield, which is not at the top of Liverpool's pre-1919 stock had 84 per cent of first-time buyers. In Birmingham we may also be seeing the effects of a disinclination of white and West Indian first-time buyers to buy into Asian dominated housing markets. They therefore enter higher up, if at all. This is, however, a speculative point. Another factor may well be the extreme dearth of mortgages in Soho and Saltley. We will be exploring this point later (Chapter 5).

THE HOUSES PURCHASED

All five areas were roughly similar in the physical characteristics of their housing, in that the majority of properties were pre-1919 terraced houses (Figures 1-7). Handsworth is an exception in that 46 per cent of the properties were post-1919, mostly inter-war. This also meant that in Handsworth a significant minority of properties (30 per cent) was semi-detached rather than terraced houses.

There were other less marked variations. In Anfield, there was a much larger proportion of dwellings which opened directly on to the street (Table 2.7). On this criterion the dwellings in Liverpool were of a lower standard than those in Birmingham. However, it was much more common for property to be built in this way in Merseyside and the Greater Manchester area, so the fact that a house opens directly on to

Table 2.7
Dwelling Characteristics by Area 1975-9

Property characteristics	Birmingham areas				All 4 B'ham areas weighted total	Liverpool Anfield
	Saltley	Soho	Sparkhill	Handsworth		
	%	%	%	%	%	%
age of property:						
pre-1919	98	91	98	54	85	92
1919-39	1	8	2	39	12	6
post-1939	1	1	-	7	3	2
Don't know	-	-	-	-	-	-
type:						
terraced	92	91	97	62	85	88
semi/end terrace	4	6	3	30	11	12
other,incl. flat & shop	4	3	-	8	4	-
front garden/space	72	89	82	89	82	40
street front	28	11	18	12	18	60
No. of storeys: 1	1	-	-	1	-	-
2	99	92	97	95	96	89
3 or more	1	8	3	4	4	11
cellar: yes	13	27	9	21	17	24
no	86	69	89	79	81	74
don't know	2	4	2	1	2	2
entrance into:						
hall	54	71	54	69	61	70
front room with porch	5	1	8	-	3	21
into front room without porch	39	28	39	26	34	8
other	2	-	-	5	2	1
(Weighted) N=	168	170	155	130	769	213

Source: Survey.

the street does not mark it out as being so clearly at the bottom end of the stock as it does in Birmingham. For instance, in Sparkhill, there is a noticeable upward gradation in property quality away from the city centre, from the Greet Housing Action Area in the north where much of the property opens on to the street, to houses with front gardens and in leafy streets in the south. Similarly in Saltley there is a marked difference in quality between the older houses closer to the city centre and opening on to the street in George Arthur Road, away to more recently-built 'villa type' terraces in the east.

One of the differences between the Liverpool houses of this type and those in Birmingham is that the Liverpool properties generally have a hall or porch which separates the living space from the street. Only 8 per cent of Liverpool houses in our sample had a front door opening straight into the front living room, compared with 34 per cent of Birmingham houses, and 39 per cent in Saltley and Sparkhill. However, partly because so much of the Anfield housing opens on to the street, in visual terms much of it does appear more cramped than in the Birmingham areas, especially in the northern part around the football ground. The only other differences between areas were the larger numbers of three storey houses in Anfield (9 per cent) and Soho (14 per cent) than in any other area, and the larger proportions of houses with cellars in Anfield (24 per cent), Soho (27 per cent) and Handsworth (21 per cent). As houses opening on to the street are unpopular with building societies, and there are reports (e.g. McIntosh, 1978) that houses with cellars and three storeys are unpopular too, these were points worth noting.

Internally there were more marked and measurable differences in the quality of the properties in Anfield and Birmingham. More houses bought in Anfield lacked one or more basic amenities (Table 2.8). In inner Birmingham 10 per cent of houses bought by recent buyers lacked a bath or shower compared with 30 per cent in Anfield. Similarly 9 per cent of houses in inner Birmingham lacked an inside toilet compared with 30 per cent in Anfield. Anfield even compared poorly with Saltley, the worst inner Birmingham survey area in terms of housing conditions, where 16 per cent of households lacked a bath or shower and 14 per cent lacked an inside toilet.

In Birmingham, the surveys showed up considerable improvements in the amenities of the houses bought in 1975-79 as compared with those bought in 1972-4. This was particularly noticeable in Soho where the proportion lacking a bath or shower was reduced to less than half (from 17 per cent to 7 per cent), as was the proportion lacking an inside toilet (21 per cent to 8 per cent). In Saltley the improvement was far less marked; the corresponding figures were, for a bath, 23 per cent to 16 per cent and, for an inside toilet, 19 per cent to 14 per cent. Sparkhill's houses already had such high levels of basic amenities that no great change was observed except in the installation of central heating. One has to remember here, as elsewhere, that we are talking about the characteristics of houses that sold in the two periods, not changes in the same houses. In theory, a picture of improving conditions could have been produced by lower rates of sale of properties with poor amenities, without any general improvement in the levels of amenity in owner-occupied properties in the survey areas.

Plate 2.1   Unimproved Properties; Opening Straight onto the street,
           A. Gough Road, Sparkhill, B. Tenby Street, Anfield

Plate 2.2 Typical Conditions of (a) Roofs and (b) Rear Extensions,
          Birmingham

Plate 2.3 Houses with small front 'gardens'
A. Dacey Rd, Anfield   B. George Arthur Rd, Saltley

Table 2.8
Facilities Lacking, by Area 1972-5 and 1979/80

| | Percent of households lacking:- | | | | | |
| | Bath or Shower | | Inside Toilet | | Central Heating | |
	1972-4	1975-9	1972-4	1975-9	1972-4	1975-9
	%	%	%	%	%	%
Saltley	23	16	19	14	95	89
Soho	17	7	21	8	95	95
Sparkhill	4	8	6	8	97	88
Handsworth	NA	5	NA	6	NA	76
Inner Birmingham						
Weighted Total	NA	10	NA	9	NA	89
Liverpool, Anfield	NA	30	NA	30	NA	93

Source: Survey.

However, a comparison of 1971 and 1981 Census data for these areas shows marked improvements in amenities.

To return to our comparison of the five areas, it is clear that housing bought by recent buyers in Anfield was considerably inferior in a number of respects to that bought in Birmingham. On the other hand, the standard of construction of houses in Anfield was probably superior to that in Birmingham, notably in terms of the quality of brick used and in the condition of the roofing.

The freehold/leasehold position in Birmingham also changed markedly between the 1974 and 1979 surveys. In Soho, Saltley and Sparkhill the overall proportion of properties that were freehold, rose from about half of those sold in 1972-4 to nearly three-quarters in 1975-9. This must partly reflect extensive conversion of leaseholds to freeholds but it may also reflect the declining marketability of leasehold houses as their leases grow shorter and conventional lenders refuse to give mortgages on them. This will either prevent a sale at all or result in a conversion to freehold. The exception which proves the rule is Saltley where leasehold sales remained at 45 per cent of all sales. But these buyers were largely Pakistanis, buying with short-term loans often from friends (Table 3.7) and therefore able to buy despite the attitudes of conventional lenders to short leases. Thus in Saltley the percentage of leases sold which had under 20 years remaining rose from 16 per cent in 1972-74 to no fewer than 57 per cent in 1975-79.

The percentage of freehold property in Anfield was 76 per cent, the same as the average for inner Birmingham (Table 2.9). However, the average for Birmingham was reduced by the small proportion of freehold property in Saltley; only 55 per cent of the property bought between 1975 and 1979 was freehold. In effect, the percentage of leasehold property in Anfield was very similar to that in Handsworth (79 per cent freehold) and Soho (83 per cent), higher than that in Saltley and lower than that in Sparkhill. As leases present a problem for conventional lenders, we would expect Anfield to have less difficulties in this respect than does Saltley but to have more problems than Sparkhill.

Table 2.9
Freehold Property by Area, 1972/74 and 1975/79

	Percentage of property freehold	
	1972–74	1975–79
	%	%
Saltley	28	55
Soho	61	83
Sparkhill	70	93
Saltley, Soho and Sparkhill	48	73
Handsworth	NA	79
Birmingham (weighted average)	NA	76
Liverpool, Anfield	NA	76

Source: Survey.

BUYERS AND PROPERTIES: THE MAIN QUESTIONS

What questions do these findings regarding the characteristics of the buyers and the properties they bought raise for the main theme of this study, namely the nature and operation of home ownership in the inner city.

First, one must note the very restricted range of buyers in these areas, largely manual workers, mainly from the area itself and usually first-time buyers. Second-time buyers were common only amongst the Asians. Similarly there were few buyers coming from further afield to purchase, except amonst the Asians. Does this have a noticeable effect on demand, and hence on prices? The implication of comparing the data from 1972-4 with that from 1975-79 was that demand from outside the inner city was in fact falling further. Second, one might ask whether the rather poorer quality of the stock in Liverpool had a noticeable effect on lending. Third, there is the question of whether ethnic minorities adopt different strategies about buying. Clearly having more second-time buyers amongst the Asians already suggests that either their attitudes to the areas are different or they are more constrained in their ability to move or both. Fourth, our expectations of relatively low incomes were confirmed. In the rest of this book we are specifically considering the nature of low income home-ownership in the inner cities. In the next chapter we will be relating these features to questions about prices, financing and the process of buying.

NOTES

(1) The interviewing in Anfield took place slightly later than in Birmingham. This has to be borne in mind when incomes are compared.

3 Buying in the inner city: a good investment?

In surveys of tenure preferences, the two reasons most commonly given for buying as opposed to renting are independence and investment value, the benefits of 'capital gains'. Owners are very conscious that buying has financial advantages over renting in that they have 'something to show' for their monthly or weekly payments (See below Chapter 4). Given the importance of this financial incentive, if it were to be found that 'capital gains' in inner city areas were lower than elsewhere, this would have very important implications for the buyers there. It would be likely to affect not only their financial position, but also their opportunity to trade-up because they could not accumulate such a substantial downpayment from the equity on their present house. It would also have implications for the attitudes of lenders towards these areas. We will now consider this very important aspect of the study : house prices. The data collected for all five areas for the period 1974 to 1979, and even more so for the three Birmingham areas for 1972 to 1979, provide us with an excellent opportunity to study the changes in house prices as well as price differentials between areas.

Table 3.1 shows mean house prices in each area for each year between 1975 and 1979, and for Saltley, Soho and Sparkhill for 1972 to 1979. Also given are mean house prices for properties mortgaged by building societies in the West Midlands, the North West Region and the United Kingdom during the same years. A number of points should be noted from this table. First, compared with the average for the four Birmingham areas, the 1979 mean price for houses in Anfield was low. In 1979, a figure of £5,676 was recorded for Anfield in contrast with £6,720 for the four Birmingham areas. Anfield's 1979 prices fell somewhere between Saltley or Soho (£5,161 and £5,023 respectively) and Sparkhill (£6,774). In fact, Anfield's prices performed very similarly to Saltley's between 1975 and 1979. Each experienced stable prices in 1976-77 but then a rapid increase in 1978 and 1979. The period of stagnation lasted longer in Sparkhill and Handsworth, where prices did not 'take off' until 1979. In Soho there was an actual decline in prices so that prices in 1977 and 1978 were below their 1975 level and even in 1979 they only reached the 1976 level. In Anfield where interviewing carried on into 1980, the very high mean price for purchases in that year reflects the general rise in house prices which took place at that time, both nationally and, even more so, in the North West Region (Table 3.1).

The second point of interest is that these differences in house price performance have changed the relative price positions of the study areas between 1972 and 1979 and even between 1975 and 1979. In 1972 the mean price of houses bought was highest in Soho, followed by

Table 3.1

Area and Regional House Price Trends 1972-1979

Year	Saltley Mean price £	Saltley cum. % 1972=100	Saltley cum. % 1975=100	Soho Mean price £	Soho cum. % 1972=100	Soho cum. % 1975=100	Sparkhill Mean price £	Sparkhill cum. % 1972=100	Sparkhill cum. % 1975=100	Handsworth Mean price £	Handsworth cum. % 1975=100	All 4 Areas Mean price £	All 4 Areas cum. % 1975=100	West Midlands Mean price £	W. Mids cum. % 1972=100	W. Mids cum. % 1975=100	Liverpool Anfield Mean price £	Liverpool cum. % 1975=100	North West Region Mean price £	N.W. cum. % 1972=100	N.W. cum. % 1975=100	United Kingdom Mean price £	U.K. cum. % 1972=100	U.K. cum. % 1975=100
1972	2348	100	67	2746	100	59	2606	100	54	-	-	-	-	6232	100	57	-	-	5724	100	59	7374	100	63
1973	2840	121	81	3066	112	66	4232	162	87	-	-	-	-	8775	141	81	-	-	7836	137	80	9942	135	84
1974	3268	139	93	3322	121	72	4788	184	99	-	-	-	-	10252	165	94	-	-	8890	155	91	10990	149	93
1975	3513	150	100	4636	169	100	4839	186	100	5953	100	4684	100	10866	174	100	3900	100	9971	174	100	11787	160	100
1976	3932	168	112	4940	180	107	5367	206	111	6915	116	5072	108	11621	186	107	4384	112	10500	183	107	12704	172	108
1977	3915	167	111	4540	165	98	5268	202	109	6731	113	4964	106	12528	201	115	4380	112	11523	201	118	13650	185	115
1978	4396	187	125	4389	160	95	5489	211	113	6802	114	5157	110	14342	230	132	5115	131	13410	234	137	15594	212	132
1979	5161	220	147	5023	183	108	6774	260	140	8617	145	6720	143	18493	297	170	5676	146	16902	295	173	19925	270	169
1980	-	-	-	-	-	-	-	-	-	-	-	-	-	21663	347	199	7929	203	20920	365	214	23596	319	200

Areas as % of Regional Mean

Year	Saltley	Soho	Sparkhill	Handsworth	All 4 Areas	West Midlands	Liverpool Anfield	North West Region	U.K. % West Mids.	U.K. % North West
1972	38	44	42	-	-	100	-	100	118	129
1975	32	42	45	55	43	100	40	100	108	121
1979	28	27	36	47	36	100	34	100	108	118

Source: Survey and Building Societies Association and Department of Environment 5 per cent sample survey of building society mortgage completions, BSA Bulletin No. 29, Jan. 1982.

Sparkhill and then Saltley. By 1975 average house prices in Soho had fallen below those of Sparkhill and, by 1979, Soho had become the area with the lowest mean house prices. Meanwhile Sparkhill house prices had risen to considerably higher levels than those in both Saltley and Soho. House prices in those two areas were roughly comparable. Also in 1972 the mean house price in the most expensive area was only 11 per cent higher than in the cheapest area. By 1979 not only had the order of areas changed, but the gap widened so that mean prices in the most expensive area were now 35 per cent higher than in the cheapest area. The more rapid rise in Sparkhill indicates the extent to which differences between 'upmarket' and 'downmarket' areas are emerging and widening within the inner city.

The third point to note about Table 3.1 is that in the period 1975 to 1979 mean house prices in all the study areas inflated at a slower rate than those in the West Midlands, the North West Region or the country as a whole. In that period prices rose 69 per cent in the country as a whole, 70 per cent in the West Midlands and 73 per cent in the North West Region. In contrast Saltley's prices rose only 47 per cent, Anfield's 46 per cent, Handsworth's 45 per cent, Sparkhill's 40 per cent and Soho's 8 per cent. Overall prices in the four Birmingham areas increased by 43 per cent.

For Saltley, Soho and Sparkhill we are able to see the price changes over the whole period 1972 to 1979. Again in all these areas the prices inflated at a slower rate than in the West Midlands or the country as a whole. Thus nationally prices inflated 170 per cent between 1972 and 1979, and in the West Midlands 197 per cent. In comparison Sparkhill's prices rose only 160 per cent, Saltley's 120 per cent and Soho's 83 per cent. Clearly Soho has experienced a particularly marked stagnation, especially in the period since 1975.

The result of this lower rate of inflation has been that all the inner city areas have lost value relative to their surrounding regional average. The drop between 1972 and 1974 in the mean area prices as a percentage of regional price has been from 38 to 28 per cent in Saltley, from 44 to 27 per cent in Soho and, even in Sparkhill, from 42 to 36 per cent. In the 1975 to 1979 period the decline has been from 32 to 28 per cent in Saltley, from 42 to 27 per cent in Soho, from 45 to 36 per cent in Sparkhill, from 55 to 47 per cent in Handsworth and from 40 to 34 per cent in Anfield. At least over the period studied inner city house prices seem to have been declining relative to the more expensive suburbs, widening the price gap between them.

Two points need to be considered in relation to these trends in Birmingham. The first is that there has been a decline in sitting tenant purchases. The second is that the proportion of leasehold sales has declined (Table 2.9). Both these factors might be expected to result in Birmingham's inner city areas experiencing a greater rather than a smaller increase in house prices. In fact, sitting tenant purchases were too few to have had any overall impact on price trends, though they did have an impact on particular ethnic groups (see Table 3.5 and accompanying text). Certainly declining numbers of leasehold sales had an impact on prices; but the effects were not simple. In general one would expect average prices to rise as the proportion of leasehold property fell. However, in Saltley, a very

Table 3.2 : Area and Regional House Price Trends : Freehold and Leasehold Property Cumulative % Increases

	Saltley		Soho		Sparkhill		West Midlands	United Kingdom
	Freehold	Freehold and leasehold	Freehold	Freehold and leasehold	Freehold	Freehold and leasehold	Freehold and leasehold	Freehold and leasehold
1972	100	100	100	100	100	100	100	100
1973	157	121	107	112	156	162	141	135
1974	142	139	108	121	180	184	165	149
1975	160	150	156	169	176	186	174	160
1976	177	168	165	180	200	206	186	172
1977	181	167	151	165	193	202	201	185
1978	200	187	144	160	201	211	230	212
1979	253	220	167	183	252	260	297	270

Source: Survey and BSA/DOE Survey

Table 3.3
Prices of Pre-1919 Terraced Houses compared with prices in Inner Birmingham and Liverpool 1977-1979

	Birmingham and Liverpool			Inner city survey area prices as percentage of Abbey National prices		
	1977	1978	1979	1977	1978	1979
	£	£	£	%	%	%
Average price[x]						
Saltley	3,915	4,396	5,161	50	48	42
Soho	4,540	4,389	5,023	59	48	41
Sparkhill	5,268	5,489	6,774	68	60	56
Handsworth	6,731	6,802	8,617	87	74	71
Anfield	4,380	5,115	5,676	66	61	56

	1977 (last quarter)	1978 (last quarter)	1979 (last quarter)
Pre 1919 terraced houses mortgaged by Abbey National[+]	£	£	£
West Midlands	7,753	9,138	12,174
North West	6,676	8,357	10,050

+ Source: Abbey National Building Society: Homes, People, Prices and Places Nos 1-18.

x Source: Survey.

sharp decline in the price of the remaining leasehold property, as the leases grew shorter, cancelled out the effect of increases in the price of property being converted to freehold.

In Soho and Sparkhill, however, freehold prices rose less rapidly than the increase of leasehold and freehold property combined. This was partly because of the falling proportion of leasehold property and partly because those leasehold properties that did sell were closer to the price of freehold property in 1979 than they were in 1972. This may have been because they had relatively longer leases or were larger properties, or perhaps because the continuing demand for leasehold property amongst buyers with unconventional finance bid the price up. So a falling level of leasehold sales is a safe predictor neither of rising nor of falling prices.

A further and more detailed comparison of trends can be made for the period 1975-1979 using DOE/Inland Revenue data for Birmingham district. The average price of all second-hand dwellings in Birmingham was £9,100 in 1975, £10,581 in 1976, £11,680 in 1977, £13,686 in 1978 and £15,872 in 1979. As will be apparent from a comparison with Table 3.1, the average price for Birmingham was much lower than that for the West Midlands. However despite the differential the same trend emerges – with the survey areas falling in price relative to the Birmingham average. Thus in 1975 the indices for the four areas, Sparkhill, Soho, Saltley and Handsworth stood at 49, 47, 36 and 60 as a percentage of the Birmingham average. In 1979 they were 43, 32, 32 and 54 respectively.

Another question worth asking is whether the price trends of these inner city properties are those which apply to all pre-1919 property in the region or whether those located in the inner city have had smaller increases. Statistics provided by the Abbey National Building Society allow us to compare the prices of the pre-1919 property upon which this building society lends with the prices of property in our survey areas. We find from this comparison (Table 3.3) that the average prices of pre-1919 houses mortgaged by the Abbey National in the West Midlands and North West regions gained in value relative to the prices of the houses sold in our survey areas. Saltley's price fell from 50 per cent of the Abbey National mean in 1977 to 42 per cent in 1979. For the other areas the figures were as follows: Soho, 59 per cent to 41 per cent; Sparkhill 68 per cent to 56 per cent; Handsworth (with more inter-war property) 87 per cent to 71 per cent and Anfield from 65 per cent to 56 per cent.

The pattern then is firmly established: localised decline amidst more general growth, requiring that we recognise the levels of differentiation which exist. This would fit with what we know about the decline of inner city areas in other respects during the 1970s, in such matters as the increasing concentrations of poorly paid unskilled workers, high rates of unemployment, and other indices of deprivation. But, as we have seen, the inner cities are not an undifferentiated mass of housing. Different parts of the inner city have been reacting in different ways. In particular we found that the newer, better standard housing in the outer margins of the inner city has been increasing in value faster than the older housing. Housing action areas also seem to have lost value relative to other areas. For instance, in Sparkhill, prices in the Greet Housing Action Area fell relative to the Sparkhill mean, from 83 per cent in 1975 to 76 per cent in 1979. In Anfield the fall was more dramatic, with prices falling in the housing action area from 95 per cent of the Anfield mean in 1975 to only 77 per cent in 1979 (Table 3.4). Thus, while in the non-housing action areas of Anfield house prices rose by 72 per cent, in the housing action area they rose by only 18 per cent. It was only this very low rate of increase in the housing action area which made the inflation rate in the whole Anfield area so much lower than that in the North West Region (73 per cent).

The same sorts of differences appeared in the inflation rate of inter-war and pre-1919 properties. In Handsworth in 1975, pre-1919 houses sold for 80 per cent, on average, of the price of newer property, but by 1979 the proportion had fallen to 62 per cent, because pre-1919 houses had inflated by only 27 per cent compared with 63 per cent for the newer houses.

In Birmingham there were also marked differences between the prices paid by the various ethnic groups (Table 3.5). Excluding sitting tenant buyers, (because they were almost entirely British and Irish and bought at discount prices), the mean prices paid by the different ethnic groups were as follows, in descending order of prices: West Indian £7,790, East African Asian £6,404, British and Irish £6,246, Indian £5,454 and Pakistani £4,429. The much higher prices paid by West Indians partly reflect their heavy concentration in our sample in the inter-war stock in Handsworth, the most expensive area surveyed. The high prices paid by the British and Irish and East African Asians also partly reflect their concentration in Sparkhill, the next most expensive of the surveyed areas. White buyers were not paying the highest prices in all areas though. They were paying the most in Saltley and Handsworth but not in Sparkhill where Asians have been

Table 3.4
Mean Area House Price by Year and Type of Area; Anfield, Liverpool

Year	Total mean price	Total cumulative increase (1975=100)	Non-HAA mean price	Non-HAA cumulative increase (1975=100)	HAA mean price	HAA cumulative increase (1975=100)
	£	%	£	%	£	%
1975	3,900	100	3,991	100	3,717	100
1976	4,384	112	4,770	120	3,656	98
1977	4,380	112	5,563	139	2,436	66
1978	5,115	131	5,732	144	4,140	112
1979	5,676	146	6,851	172	4,391	118
1980	7,929	203	8,437	211	6,492	175
Weighted Total	5,277		6,073		4,038	

Source: Survey.

Table 3.5
Mean House Prices by Country of Birth and Year
(Excluding Sitting Tenant Purchasers) : Birmingham

	1975	% of 1975	1976	% of 1975	1977	% of 1975	1978	% of 1975	1979	% of 1975	1975-79
	£	%	£	%	£	%	£	%	£	%	£
British & Ulster & Eire	4,732	100	5,892	112	5,815	123	6,230	132	7,426	157	6,246
Pakistan	3,690	100	4,151	112	4,058	110	4,472	121	5,444	148	4,429
Indian	4,813	100	5,223	109	5,108	126	4,944	102	6,771	141	5,454
W. Indian	5,634	100	6,955	123	6,980	124	6,705	119	10,389	184	7,790
E. African	6,150	100	6,325	103	6,047	98	6,957	113	8,000	130	6,404
All ethnic groups	4,684	100	5,072	108	4,964	106	5,157	110	6,720	143	5,595

Source: Survey.

increasingly buying the more expensive stock. (In Soho there were so few white buyers that analysis of average prices by country of birth is not helpful).

Despite the movement of Asians into more expensive houses in Sparkhill, on average they were buying relatively cheaper houses in 1979 than in 1975 as compared with white and West Indian buyers. The trend is partly associated with the stagnation of prices in Soho where so many Indians were buying though this is not the whole explanation, because Pakistanis did not buy in Soho. We are seeing British and Irish buyers, and West Indians in particular, moving up- market in the inner city, tending to leave the cheaper stock to Asian buyers. Clearly, there are some Asians who have moved up into the more expensive stock. This is only to be expected because, as the percentage of Asian buyers continues to rise, and white buyers take smaller and smaller proportions of even the most expensive stock in the inner city, Asians will necessarily obtain more and more of the higher priced properties. This is shown most clearly in Sparkhill where there are the largest quantities of higher priced houses and where the decline in white buying has been proportionately greatest.

In summary, our evidence somewhat undermines the belief that many home owners have in the investment value of properties in the inner city. Clearly the social inequality between higher income suburban buyers with modern houses in good repair and lower income inner city buyers with old, dilapidated houses is exacerbated by the fact that the latter are in addition making smaller capital gains on their property.

Also, since two of the greatest financial advantages to owner-occupiers in Britain are that they are taxed neither on capital gains nor on the current value to them of occupying their house (i.e. the imputed rent, see Kilroy, 1978) poorer owner occupiers gain least from these two tax concessions when their property fails to keep up with general house price trends. This, combined with the fact that they gain relatively little from tax relief (see below p.   ), means that the inner city buyers in this study receive relatively little government assistance towards their housing costs as compared with higher income suburban buyers. In the case of Soho the stagnation of house prices has been such that those who bought there may well be worse off financially than if they had rented a property and invested their savings.

SOURCES OF FINANCE FOR HOUSE PURCHASE

We will now move on to consider the investment being made in the inner city by the major financial institutions in terms of finance for purchase. We will describe lending patterns in the three originally surveyed areas of Birmingham first and then go on to consider Handsworth and Anfield. One of the most important findings of the 1974 survey was that there was very little lending by building societies in inner Birmingham, where, for instance, only 8 per cent of buyers in Soho or Saltley bought with building society mortgages (Table 3.6). Even in Sparkhill, where house prices were considerably higher than in the other areas and where there was a majority of white buyers, only 36 per cent of buyers had a building society mortgage. Banks and finance companies were the largest lenders in all areas, ranging from 61 per cent of recent buyers' finance in Saltley through 44 per cent in Soho to 37 per cent in Sparkhill. This evidence of the lack of building society activity in inner Birmingham, along with other similar evidence about lending in other inner city areas and building society attitudes generally (e.g. Bassett and Short, 1980a; Boddy, 1976; Burney, 1967; Duncan, 1977; Grime and Smith, 1982; Harrison, 1979; Lambert, 1976; Melville-Ross, 1981; Weir, 1976; Williams, 1976) focussed attention upon the performance of building societies and led to some criticism that in effect building societies engage in redlining, even if they deny doing so deliberately or explicitly (Weir, 1976).

Since then, the building societies themselves have expressed more awareness of the need to move downmarket by lending on property which might previously have been thought to be too risky. Several major buildings societies have announced plans to expand lending in housing action areas and similar rundown areas of inner cities. However, as yet there has been little evidence that this has had an appreciable impact upon the overall pattern of building society lending in inner cities. It is true that the proportion of building society loans nationally going to the purchase of pre-1919 houses rose during the 1970s, from 16 per cent in 1969 to 28 per cent in 1981. However, by no means all pre-1919 property is in inner cities or is the poor, terraced type predominant in our survey areas. The disparity between inner city prices and the Abbey National's pre-1919 house prices illustrate this point very clearly (Table 3.3). It is entirely possible that up to now the increase in lending on pre-1919 property may be more due to a whole range of extraneous factors, such as the decline in new construction which has occurred over the period and the decline in additions to the owner occupied stock from private landlords, rather than any deliberate

Table 3.6 : Source of Finance by Area

Source of finance	1972 - 1974			All 3 B'ham Areas	1975 - 1979			All 3 B'ham Areas	Handsworth	All 4 B'ham Areas	Liverpool, Anfield		Whole Area
	Saltley	Soho	Sparkhill		Saltley	Soho	Sparkhill				HAA	Non HAA	
	%	%	%	%	%	%	%	%	%	%	%	%	%
Council	8	21	12	12	10	13	16	-	26	16	40	21	28
Building society or Insurance Co.	8	8	36	15	8	12	45	-	39	25	23	59	45
Bank	49	34	27	39	43	35	23	-	14	30	5	4	4
Fringe Bank/ Finance Co.	12	10	10	11	1	1	1	-	1	1	2	2	2
Vendor, Solicitor, Estate Agent etc.	2	3	1	2	4	4	-	-	1	1	10	5	7
Friend or relative	3	4	1	3	20	15	8	-	11	14	3	1	2
Cash buyer	19	21	13	19	14	21	7	-	9	13	17	8	12
Total	100	100	100	100	100	100	100		100	100	100	100	100
Weighted N=	119	104	102	-	168	170	146		130	769			213

Source: Survey

Table 3.7 : Source of Finance by Country of Birth - 1975–79

Source of Finance	Birmingham - All Four Areas							Liverpool, Anfield
	England Scotland or Wales	Ulster or Eire	Pakistan or Bangladesh	India	West Indian	East Africa	All Countries of Origin	All Countries of Origin
	%	%	%	%	%	%	%	%
Council	36	(11)	5	11	37	(8)	16	28
Building Society or Insurance Co.	32	(55)	8	20	53	(67)	25	45
Bank	7	(11)	49	36	4	(17)	30	4
Finance Co, Money Lender	1	(4)	2	5	2	-	1	2
Solicitor, Estate Agent or Vendor etc.	-	-	-	-	-	-	1	6
Friend or Relative	4	(6)	25	12	3	-	14	2
Other	-	-	-	*	-	-	-	1
Cash (no loan)	20	(13)	11	15	1	(8)	13	12
Total	100	100	100	100	100	100	100	100
Weighted N=	142	36	261	204	62	45	769	213

Source: Survey

* 0.5% or less

by the building societies to move downmarket. For a period after 1979, building societies were having also to compete for borrowers for the first time for many years and this may have affected their willingness to lend in inner areas. But the shortage of borrowers did not continue beyond 1982. Even if the shortage had continued, it is not certain that it would have had a marked effect on the inner cities; as we saw in the period 1972-74, when building society funds were freely available, building society lending was very low in inner Birmingham.

In view of these conflicting assessments of the situation, one of the key questions to which the 1979 survey of recent buyers was addressed was whether there had been any appreciable increase in building society activity in the original survey areas and what the current levels were in all five areas. The figures in Table 3.6 summarise the percentage of houses bought with different sources of finance in all the survey areas between 1975 and 1979 and for Saltley, Soho and Sparkhill between 1972 and 1974.

In 1975-9, Sparkhill and Anfield were the two areas with the highest levels of building society lending (both 45 per cent) followed by Handsworth (39 per cent). In Anfield, outside the housing action area, the level of building society lending was even higher (59 per cent), as it was among the post-1919 houses in Handsworth (76 per cent). Soho and Saltley were in a totally different position with only 8 per cent and 12 per cent respectively.

Local authority lending was also very variable. In Birmingham it was not, however, inversely related to building society lending, as one might expect it to be if it were a lending source of last resort. Instead Soho and Saltley had the lowest levels of council lending as well as the lowest levels of building society lending. Altogether, Saltley in 1979 had only 18 per cent of its finance from these two conventional sources; Soho had 25 per cent. In contrast Sparkhill had 61 per cent and Handsworth 65 per cent. In Anfield, however, there was a much more marked compensatory activity by the local authority. In the housing action area where building society lending was only 23 per cent, the local authority was lending particularly heavily (40 per cent). Because of this the total level of conventional lending was raised to 63 per cent, a high figure in comparison with Birmingham, but still far short of the 80 per cent for the parts of Anfield outside the housing action areas.

Three other major differences between Anfield and the Birmingham areas were: first, the much heavier dependence of Birmingham buyers on bank loans; second, the frequency in Birmingham of loans from friends or relatives; and, third, the greater incidence in Anfield of loans from estate agents, vendors and solicitors (Table 3.6). As we will see in more detail in Chapter 5, it appears that where buyers in Anfield had difficulties in obtaining loans, housing market professionals were more likely to organise help for them, either by giving a loan themselves or more frequently by arranging one with a building society. In both cities it is clear that the organisation of local markets follows quite specific patterns, suggesting once again the diverse and differentiated character of the national housing market, and indeed of regional and city wide markets.

From the surveys in Soho, Saltley and Sparkhill, we can examine trends since 1972 in relation to lending. Apart from Sparkhill, no areas had any significant increase in building society lending. Ironically, as we said earlier, Sparkhill also had the only significant increase in local authority lending. Since 1974 there were major reductions in local government spending on mortgage finance which had led to severe rationing of mortgages. In Birmingham rationing was conducted on the basis of a maximum price of property (£13,000 up to 1979), a system which was supposed to direct more lending towards the poorest areas. It is ironical, therefore, that it was Sparkhill, the most expensive of the three areas, which had an increase in local authority lending. Soho's local authority lending fell from 21 per cent in 1972-74 to 13 per cent in 1975-79 and Saltley's remained roughly stable at 8 per cent.

The two most notable overall changes in lending patterns in the three areas were the virtual disappearance of fringe bank lending and the massive increase in informal loans from friends or relatives. In Soho, Saltley and Sparkhill, informal loans had increased from negligible numbers in 1972-74, to over 20 per cent, 15 per cent and 8 per cent of sales in 1975-79. This change, like the use of vendors and estate agents mortgages in Anfield, suggests mortgage difficulties in these areas.

The decline in fringe bank lending was expected because of the collapse of the fringe banks in 1974-75. Clearing bank lending might also have been expected to decline because clearing bank lending for conventional term mortgages reached a peak nationally in the earlier survey period but declined sharply thereafter. However, the bank lending in these areas was not through conventional term mortgages but through short-term personal loans. In fact the amount of clearing bank lending in Sparkhill and Saltley declined only slightly between the two survey periods and in Soho it remained the same. In Saltley and Soho, the banks remained the largest single source of loans. In Sparkhill they took second place to the building societies in both periods. This pattern suggests that while the banks had indeed withdrawn their lending from more conventional areas of the mortgage market, they continued to give profitable short-term loans at the bottom of the market as before.

The continuing dominance of bank lending in Birmingham and the growth in informal loans are strongly linked to the large proportion of Asians amongst the buyers. British and West Indian buyers in Birmingham had borrowing patterns roughly resembling those of Anfield buyers (Table 3.7). In other words they relied predominantly upon local authority and building society lending, seldom borrowed from banks and even less often borrowed from relatives or friends. The Irish and the East African Asians were slightly different in that they had often borrowed from banks, in the former case mainly from the Irish banks, but they seldom had local authority loans or loans from their family or friends. The Pakistanis and Indians had very different patterns, with the Pakistanis representing the greatest contrast. For Pakistanis, banks were the biggest lenders (49 per cent), followed by friends or relatives (26 per cent) and with the building societies (8 per cent) and council (5 per cent) playing only a minor role. For Indians the position was less extreme; again banks were the largest lenders (35 per cent) but were followed by building societies (22 per cent) and the local authority (13 per cent) rather than friends and relatives (12 per cent). The very different patterns of lending in the four areas in Birmingham therefore emerge as largely the product of Asian borrowing patterns. This is not entirely true since only 30 per cent of British buyers in Birmingham received building society mortgages as compared with 45 per cent in Anfield, despite the fact that Birmingham buyers purchased properties with very markedly better amenities and of higher price.

Contrary perhaps to expectations, the banks most involved in lending to Asians were not the Asian banks but the major clearing banks. The Irish banks also played a leading role. The Asian banks on the whole lend on commercial property and are not very interested in small home loans.

We must emphasise that this is by no means a static picture. Over the period 1972 to 1979, we can observe in the Saltley, Soho and Sparkhill areas that a number of changes have appeared in the borrowing patterns of the different groups (Table 3.8). Though, overall, bank lending was maintained at roughly the same level in 1979 as in 1972-75, in fact this was the product of an absolute increase in the proportion of Asian buyers. Within the Asian groups, bank lending had declined in importance, particularly for the Pakistanis. Finance company lending had declined more dramatically, particularly for white and Pakistani buyers. West Indian and Indian buyers experienced a reduction in lending but at least 5 per cent continued to use this source. These declining sources of institutional loans have been replaced in different ways by the West Indians, Indians and Pakistanis. The Pakistanis have moved to relying very much more on friends and relatives, while West Indians and Indians obtained both more loans from friends and relatives and more building society loans. British buyers were faced with only one major shift, a decline in their ability to buy for cash. This was more than compensated for by an increase in local authority lending.

So ethnic polarisation appears to be taking place in these three Birmingham areas in terms of the financing of house purchase. In particular it is noteworthy that where there has been an increase in building society lending, it has gone largely to British/Irish (and in Soho to West Indian) buyers, with East African Asians and Indians receiving a small share. Housing finance for the growing percentage of Pakistani buyers and a large number of Indians has become even more dependent upon unconventional sources which are increasingly non-institutional.

The differences between the types of loans in terms of interest rates, loan periods and percentage of the purchase price covered were those that would be expected. Bank loans were personal loans rather than conventional mortgages and were for particularly short terms. In Birmingham 81 per cent of bank loans were for up to five years and 92 per cent for up to seven. (The surveys were, of course, carried out before the temporary increase in conventional mortgage lending by banks during the early 1980s. The 1974 survey however covered a period of very active bank lending for house purchase. Even then these inner city buyers almost invariably had personal loans. This, and the fact

Table 3.8 : Source of Finance by Country of Birth - Saltley, Soho and Sparkhill

Source of Finance	Britain and Ireland 1972-4	1975-9	Pakistan or Bangladesh 1972-4	1975-9	India 1972-4	1975-9	West Indies 1972-4	1975-9	East Africa 1975-9	All 1972-4	1975-9
	%	%	%	%	%	%	%	%	%	%	%
Council	16	31	3	4	16	9	(45)	33	(7)	12	13
Building Society or Insurance Co.	37	36	3	6	5	14	(24)	46	(64)	15	19
Bank	10	11	63	52	41	38	(10)	-	(21)	39	36
Fringe Bank/ Finance Co.	11	1	11	2	9	5	(16)	7	-	11	3
Vendor/Solicitor Estate Agent	3	-	1	-	2	1	-	-	-	1	*
Friend or relative	-	4	3	24	5	14	-	11	-	2	15
Cash buyer	23	18	15	11	20	19	-	4	(7)	18	14
No reply	1	-	-	-	2	-	(5)	-	-	1	-
Total	100	100	100	100	100	100	100	100	100	100	100
Weighted N=	111	121	155	263	93	210	19	77	45	396	769

Source: Survey

Table 3.9 : Head of Household's Income by Source of Finance

Net Weekly Head of Household Income	Birmingham - all areas 1979 Local Authority	Building Society	Bank	Friends or Relatives	Liverpool, Anfield, 1980 Local Authority	Building Society
	%	%	%	%	%	%
Up to £40	6	4	11	20	6	6
£41 - 50	6	9	12	7	4	8
£51 - 60	27	14	18	32	9	8
£61 - 70	21	26	25	19	13	11
£71 - 80	21	20	19	13	33	15
£81 - 90	5	14	8	4	19	18
£91 - 100	7	4	3	3	4	15
£101 and over	7	8	4	2	13	19
Total	100	100	100	100	100	100
(Weighted) N=	124	185	216	105	54	85
Mean	£68	£70	£61	£57	£77	£81

Source: Survey

that recent bank lending through conventional term mortgages has been concentrated at the top end of the market, leads us to expect little change in the character of inner city bank lending). Finance company loans were for slightly longer periods. The repayment periods of local authority and building society loans differed between Anfield and Birmingham. In inner Birmingham local authority loans were for slightly longer periods than building society loans; 58 per cent were for over twenty years compared with 36 per cent of building society mortgages. In Liverpool it was the other way round: local authority loan periods were shorter; only 10 per cent of local authority loans compared with 31 per cent of building society loans were for over twenty years.

Interest rates on short-term bank loans were, of course, much higher than those of building societies, usually about 3 per cent above the building society long-term mortgage rate. But, perhaps more interesting, was the fact that about a third of the buyers with bank, building society or local authority loans did not know what rate of interest they were currently paying. However, respondents were much clearer about their tax position. Only about 5 per cent of those with a building society or local authority loan were unclear if they had option mortgage subsidy or tax relief (this was, of course, before the introduction of MIRAS). However, those with bank loans were understandably much more confused and it appeared that a substantial minority of them, perhaps a fifth, were losing the tax relief to which they were entitled. At the very high interest rates they were paying, the sums they lost would have been considerable.

Those with informal loans from banks or relatives were not normally paying interest and, even if they had, would not have qualified for tax relief. Because they depend on informal loans so much, Asians tend not to be receiving any tax relief subsidy for owner-occupation but rather to be subsidising each other by waiving interest payments. As there is a moral obligation for the borrower to help others in a similar way at a later date, and to forego interest, the eventual financial gain to buyers is probably less than it appears. There is another and growing problem, namely, that lenders not infrequently need the loans repaid early because of their own financial problems, often due to unemployment. But the system does have the advantage of spreading expenditure away from the early years of ownership and of producing a 'non-profit' lending system which reduces the cost of buying for all participants. It resembles, though normally in a less organised form, the original terminating building societies, with members taking turns to draw capital from a pool. It is ironic that the credit needs of today's working class should lead them to continuously 're-invent' the building societies, when the building societies themselves have developed far from their original roots.

As has been repeatedly pointed out elsewhere, the system of mortgage tax relief gives the greatest subsidy to those with the highest incomes and, within the £25,000 limit at that time, the largest loans (e.g. Department of Environment 1977, Technical Vol 1 p 214). In this study, building society borrowers had the highest incomes and largest loans of all buyers, followed closely by local authority mortgagors (Table 3.9). Bank borrowers had lower incomes and those with loans from friends and relations the lowest of all. It will be recalled that only four fifths of bank borrowers were likely to claim their tax relief subsidy and those with informal loans received no subsidies at all.

There was a strong relationship between type of finance and house price. Table 3.10 shows the mean house price by type of finance in all five areas. It can be seen that the mean price of houses bought with building society mortgages was higher than the mean price of houses bought with any other type of finance in every area in both 1972-1974 and 1975-1979. It is also notable that, despite both councils' policies of lending on lower priced houses, the mean price of houses bought with council mortgages was above the mean for the area in both Saltley and Soho and close to the mean in Sparkhill and Anfield. Finally, the mean price of houses bought outright was considerably lower than the mean for all houses in all five areas in all years.

The considerable variation in the price of houses bought with different sources of finance is brought out more clearly if we consider the percentage of buyers who bought houses priced above the mean for the area. For instance, among those who borrowed from friends and relatives only 27 per cent in Saltley, 32 per cent in Soho, 9 per cent in Sparkhill and none in Anfield bought houses prices above the area mean. The next lowest category was those buying for cash and without a loan: 12 per cent in Anfield, 29 per cent in both Sparkhill and Soho, and 30 per cent in Saltley bought houses priced above the area mean. In contrast, buyers with council mortgages more often bought houses priced above the mean: 71 per cent in Saltley, 55 per cent in Soho, though only 48 per cent in Anfield and 38 per cent in Sparkhill. However, the overwhelming majority of those buying with building society mortgages bought houses priced above the mean; 73 per cent in Anfield, 85 per cent in both Soho and Sparkhill and no less than 93 per cent of buyers in Saltley.

The picture of lending produced here is in line with the results of Liverpool City Council's own examination of Support Lending. In 1978 the Council's housing strategy statement (Liverpool City Council, 1978) reported as follows:-

The Council's experience of the Building Societies Lending Support Scheme is that, while it is a useful supplement to direct local authority lending, it is not yet a substitute since the building societies' lending criteria (and their valuers' assessments) tend to deny mortgage loans in many of the present and proposed priority areas. Most of the local societies appear to exclude older properties with a purchase price of less than £4,500 (even £6,000 in one case). They are generally unwilling to lend on unimproved property (even with agreement that an improvement grant would be given) and some societies seem to specifically exclude 'Inner City' areas. Furthermore, the societies do not advance 100 per cent mortgages, which are required by many of the less-well-off applicants. Liaison with the building societies has not, so far, indicated major changes in their attitudes.

Table 3.10 : Source of Finance by Mean House Price

Source of Finance	Saltley 1972-1974	Saltley 1975-1979	Soho 1972-1974	Soho 1975-1979	Sparkhill 1972-1974	Sparkhill 1975-1979	Handsworth 1975-1979	Anfield 1975-1979
	£	£	£	£	£	£	£	£
Cash buyer	2700	3319	2463	3929	2721	4630	6125	3117
Local Authority loan	2654	5218	2865	4702	2956	5382	6937	5144
Building Society or Insurance Co.	3317	6161	3681	5862	4313	6586	8615	6636
Bank	2571	4378	3127	4892	4173	4446	8013	3415
Finance Co.	(3962)	(2775)	(3640)	(5275)	(3685)	(2500)	(4750)	-
Vendor, solicitor or other	(3633)	(3467)	(-)	(3733)	(2300)	-	(2000)	(3962)
Friend or relative	2117	3544	1962	4446	4100	4286	4523	(2500)
Area Mean	2830	4260	2986	4678	3804	5553	7364	5277
N =	116	166	104	170	102	146	129	212

Source: Survey

Since then the position has improved. In 1980/81 the City Council made a new arrangement with three building societies to concentrate advances in specified housing action areas. This arrangement has raised the proportion of Support Lending going to renewal areas from 6 per cent in 1979/80 to 34 per cent in 1980/81 (Liverpool City Planning Department, 1981). It is not clear, however, whether this increase replaces, or is in addition to, the lending which these building societies normally did on pre-1919 stock outside renewal areas (Liverpool City Planning Department, written communication). In addition, it is still the case that building society support loans are on average granted on houses with higher prices than those mortgaged by the council. The withdrawal of council mortgages in the late 1970s and 1980s has therefore left a gap which has probably depressed house prices in the housing action areas where council lending was concentrated.

The general picture to emerge concerning housing finance in these inner areas is that there has been a clear process of polarisation of sources of lending according to the price of the house and, in Birmingham, according to ethnic group. Building society lending has grown principally at the top end of the market, for instance, in the more modern part of Sparkhill. Therefore, despite building society statements about their willingness to lend in inner cities, their lending is still heavily concentrated on the most modern property, the highest priced houses, and the highest income buyers. This concentration is accentuating the process of differentiation between the up-market inner city areas in Birmingham and Liverpool and the poorer areas, with more deteriorated houses, lower income buyers and, in the case of Birmingham, Asian buyers. Lack of conventional lending may also reduce prices in the areas which already contain the cheaper, older property and therefore increase the price polarisation between areas. While, theoretically, low prices should be helpful to low income buyers in bringing property within their price-range, in practice low, and especially relatively declining, prices deter the lending institutions upon which most buyers are dependent for their access to home-ownership. So low income buyers tend to be caught between the devil of rising prices and the deep blue sea of mortgage problems. Also once a house has been bought, falling or stagnant prices offer no advantages to the owner. They reduce the value of the financial asset and of the exemption from capital gains and imputed rent taxes. They make the house more difficult to sell, because of justifiable doubts on the part of potential buyers and lenders. They make the possibility of trading-up to better quality property more problematic. And in the case of properties with a large percentage loan, stagnant prices can easily lead to a buyer who falls into arrears owing more than the price for which the house would sell (Karn, 1983b). At this point inner city home ownership even becomes a poor risk for the lending institutions, hence their unwillingness to grant large percentage loans.

4 Searching for a home

This chapter is concerned with understanding the manner in which the bottom end of the owner-occupied market operates. Market processes in the owner-occupied sector as a whole are well-understood at a very general level. Most property exchanges follow a fairly clear sequence of procedures, involving estate agents, solicitors, building societies and other institutions geared to the owner-occupied market. After finding a property, a prospective buyer will offer a price to the estate agent or vendor. Before or after that, he/she will have applied to a lending institution, normally a building society, for a mortgage and will have arranged for a solicitor to manage the transaction. This highly formal system, involving a number of different 'exchange professionals', requires considerable social skill and competence for it to be managed effectively by the buyer and the vendor. Even well-educated buyers and vendors frequently find themselves ill-informed about prices and about the way building societies operate, yet feel uncertain too about the quality of advice being offered them by professionals. Many feel at the mercy of agents and solicitors rather than trusting them implicitly to pursue the transaction in their best interests. How much more difficult then is the process of buying when most buyers are poorly educated and/or have poor knowledge of the English language and British institutions, are predominantly first time buyers and come from backgrounds in which owner-occupation has not been the normal tenure and, in Birmingham, from ethnic groups for whom the cultural, social and economic experience of buying in Britain will often be quite alien.

The contrast between such buyers and the white middle class buyer in Britain is acute. The situation is further compounded when we consider the types of property involved. The middle class buyer will normally be well placed in the housing market. He or she will have acceptable housing and is unlikely to be in a situation of panic buying.

This is far from the case with inner city buyers who seldom have self-contained property prior to buying (Table 2.5) and are often from poor, overcrowded living conditions. On top of all these problems there are the complications of inner city buying: difficulties in getting a building society mortgage when one is buying an old house or one with a short lease; lenders attitudes to low or insecure incomes; the uncertainties attached to potential local authority activities, such as the declaration of housing action areas, clearance areas and other measures to remedy unfitness. All this must mean a greater chance that a prospective buyer who has made a suitable offer will withdraw, either because he/she is refused finance or because he himself begins to have doubts about the property.

The relationships between vendors, agents and prospective buyers, which are problematic at all levels of the market, must therefore be all the more difficult in the inner cities because of the added uncertainties. On the vendor's side there will be the fear of being 'let down' by the prospective buyer. On the prospective buyer's side there will be the fear of being 'gazumped'. An agent too runs the risk of having to carry the costs of a number of unsuccessful attempts to sell in order to get his fee on completion. Solicitors too will worry about the loss of conveyancing fees if sales fall through. Since all the parties to the transaction are likely to behave in ways that they perceive as minimising their expense and risks, the total effect may well be that the operation of inner city house sale transactions are in important respects, different from the conventional suburban model where the processes of buying are more routine. To develop a comprehensive analysis of market structure, we would ideally have used data on households who had tried to buy but had failed and on vendors' as well as purchasers' activities. In this analysis, however, we are able to draw only on the experiences of households who succeeded in buying, although this is supplemented by data on the previous attempts of these households to buy, prior to the ultimate purchase.

In the previous chapter we saw the way in which the owner-occupied market in the inner city was becoming increasingly differentiated between the bottom - with more stagnant house prices and poor levels of conventional lending - and the outer newer streets with greater price inflation and more liberal lending. In association with these processes, we also saw how the class and ethnic composition of buyers in inner city areas has changed. Buyers have been sorting themselves into the differentiated stock of dwellings according to their ethnic origins, relative socio-economic status and incomes. We now go on to examine the manner in which this sorting takes place, by considering the nature of the processes through which 'successful' buyers insert themselves into the inner city housing market.

The process of buying can be very roughly divided into three phases: the initial decision to buy rather than rent, the search for a suitable and affordable property, and finally, for those without the cash for an outright purchase, the search for finance. The strategies adopted and the problems which arise vary between different groups of buyers. We consider in this chapter the decision to buy and the search for a property, and in the next chapter the search for a loan.

DECIDING TO BUY

The first issue of interest is the motivation for buying. At the income level of the buyers in our survey areas, (on average £60 to £80 a week net head of household income in 1979) it is by no means an automatic decision to buy rather than rent; in fact in 1979, only about 30 per cent of non-elderly couples with or without children and with gross incomes under £80 per week owned their houses. (Family Expenditure Survey, 1979). For those with gross incomes between £80 and £100 the comparable figure was 47 per cent. So our buyers' incomes were at the margin between buying and renting. Had they in fact considered renting? They were asked this, and in response 18 per cent in Birmingham and 24 per cent in Liverpool said they had (Table 4.1).

The difference between the cities is explained by the very small percentage of Asian buyers who had considered renting; only 12 per cent of Pakistanis, 14 per cent of Indians and 18 per cent of East African Asians had considered renting as compared with 29 per cent of non-Irish British and 25 per cent of West Indian buyers. Furthermore only 5 per cent of Pakistanis had actually tried to rent but failed, compared with more than double that proportion of Indians (12 per cent) and more than four times the proportion of British and West Indians (24 per cent and 23 per cent respectively).

So it is the case that in each city about a quarter of the white and West Indian buyers and about a seventh of other buyers had considered renting and a large proportion of those who had considered renting had tried to do so, but without success. 'Rented housing', of course, means essentially local authority housing because there is so little privately rented housing, in particular unfurnished privately rented housing suitable for families. In Birmingham, even in 1971, only 19 per cent of the stock was rented from a private landlord or housing association. By 1981 the 19 per cent had fallen to 13 per cent. In Liverpool there was more privately rented housing but the decline was more dramatic. In 1971 there was 32 per cent private rented stock. By 1981 the total private rental figure had fallen to 20 per cent (1981 Census, County Monitors). It is therefore not surprising that buyers had given little consideration to private renting; only 11 per cent in Liverpool and 5 per cent in Birmingham had considered private renting, and 7 per cent in Liverpool and 2 per cent in Birmingham had considered a housing association, totals of 18 per cent and 7 per cent respectively. The greater awareness of housing associations in Liverpool probably reflects the very active (and high profile) role of several very large associations in the inner city, a role strongly encouraged by the local authority.

Because 36 per cent of the whole housing stock in Liverpool and Birmingham in 1971 consisted of council housing, a much larger proportion of buyers said they had considered council housing - 21 per cent of buyers in Liverpool and 15 per cent in Birmingham. Why was it that those owners who only bought after failing to rent were unable to find a rented property? And why did others not consider renting when it is the majority tenure for people in their income bracket?

The explanations are linked and are a mixture of the household's urgent need to find a home, the perceived attractions of owning and the scarcity and perceived deficiencies of council housing. (Table 4.2) At the time of the survey, in both Liverpool and Birmingham it was relatively easy to gain access to council housing of some sort, as long as a family would accept a poor quality flat or maisonette in a relatively unpopular and possibly remote area. Only those who did not qualify for council housing at all were unable to obtain this sort of property. Some who did not qualify appeared in the survey, a few were disqualified because they lived outside Liverpool or Birmingham before they bought therefore failing to qualify under the residential qualification, and, some because they were previously owners, were excluded by Birmingham's rule disqualifying owner-occupiers.

Table 4.1 : Whether Buyers Considered Renting (Birmingham and Liverpool, 1979/80) Buyers Survey) By Country of Birth

Considered Renting	Birmingham (weighted data) Country of Origin								Anfield Liverpool
	England Scotland or Wales	Eire or Ulster	Pakistan or Bangladesh	India	West Indian	East Africa	Other	Total	
	%	%	%	%	%	%	%	%	%
No	71	(85)	88	85	75	(82)	68	82	76
Yes, but did not try	5	-	7	2	1	(2)	17	4	7
Yes, tried but failed	24	(15)	5	12	23	(16)	15	14	17
No reply	-	-	-	1	-	-	-	-	-
Total %	100	100	100	100	100	100	100	100	100
N (weighted =)	142	36	261	204	62	45	21	769	213
Percent of total who:-									
Considered Council Renting	24	12	9	12	21	14	24	15	21
Considered Housing Association Renting*								2	7
Considered Private Renting*								6	11

* Numbers too small for ethnic breakdown

Source: survey

Table 4.2: Reason for Buying by Country of Birth: Birmingham and Liverpool

Birmingham

	England Scotland or Wales	Ulster or Eire	Pakistan	India	West Indian	East Africa	Birmingham (weighted sample)	Anfield Liverpool
	%	%	%	%	%	%	%	%
Cheaper than or same price as renting	11	23	13	19	10	10	15	15
Investment	34	35	20	21	23	28	23	25
Hard to get council house or other rented accommodation	14	7	10	7	17	11	11	20
Freedom, privacy, security, independence	8	11	16	16	20	11	14	13
Your own house	12	8	26	24	19	33	22	13
Wanted this house in particular	11	13	4	8	2	5	7	10
Wanted house to bring family to from abroad	-	-	7	4	-	-	3	-
Other	9	3	4	1	9	2	5	4
No reply	1	-	-	-	-	-	*	-
Total	100	100	100	100	100	100	100	100
(Weighted) N =	142	36	261	204	62	45	769	213

Source: Survey

Although poorer maisonettes or flats had by the late 1970s become relatively easy to obtain, it was still difficult for a family with children to obtain a house by applying to the waiting list. Since then the position has deteriorated further. Because of the shortage of houses, families that already have children when they apply for council housing are likely to have to wait much longer if they insist on a house rather than a flat. If they are in urgent need of housing, as so many of the buyers in the survey were, they will have to trade off a longer wait against the quality of housing they will receive. This explains why so many of the buyers who said they had not considered council renting gave as their reason the fact that waiting periods were too long. In other words they had considered renting but had dismissed it as being too problematic when their need for housing was urgent. This fits in with the fact that most of the inner city buyers already had one or more children when they were looking for a house to buy or rent.

The Asians, in particular, have relatively large families and therefore face particular difficulties in obtaining good council housing. Studies of the allocation of council housing in Birmingham (Flett 1979 and Henderson and Karn, 1984) have found that most Asians request council housing in areas of the city where it is most scarce, particularly the middle ring, that when housed they receive, not purpose-built council housing but pre-1919 houses similar to the property purchased in our study and, finally, that they have to accumulate above-average numbers of points before being housed at all. For them, therefore, there may seem even fewer advantages in applying for council renting. It would be foolish to believe that the quality of housing received has no effect on potential applicants. In this study we are seeing evidence of the effect of the scarcity of good quality houses in the council sector on the ultimate tenure decisions of applicants. For example, some typical responses to the question about why they decided to buy were as follows:

'You'd have to wait that long on the housing list, you'd end up with no home at all.'

'The council only offered bad accommodation in broken-down flats.'

'In council property you have to live where they say or else you won't get a house.'

'We wanted a house and there are only flats available for rent.'

'When the old house was pulled down, my father took a council house and I bought this. We would have liked to live together but we couldn't get a council house large enough.'

A few buyers who were unhappy about the quality of council housing had in fact previously been council tenants and wanted to move out. This particularly applied to Anfield buyers who had previously lived on one of Liverpool's peripheral estates.

'We were renting from the council. There was nothing there for the children. What was there was vandalised. We wanted to get the children away from there.'

So in the eyes of many buyers, both those who tried to rent and those who did not, the council allocation process was merely likely to bring offers of poor quality housing in areas they did not want.

On the whole, as we saw earlier, Pakistanis had given little consideration to council housing, Indians only slightly more. However, this picture should not be regarded as a fixed one. Whatever their motives for buying or renting, Asians are now registering on waiting lists and being housed by local authorities on a vastly larger scale than before (Robinson, 1980; Henderson and Karn, 1984). This radically changing pattern of tenure in the Asian communities must be one of the question marks which hangs over the future viability of owner-occupied housing in inner Birmingham since Asians currently dominate the market there. If they follow the West Indians in retreating from a high rate of home-ownership in the earlier years of immigration to a pattern which resembles that of the white working class, namely a much greater use of council housing, then we have to consider a picture in which the inner city home ownership market will need an injection of totally new types of buyers or experience a high rate of voids and even abandonment. Such a picture would, however, be dependent on the willingness and ability of the public sector to meet the needs of Asian families satisfactorily, a condition which is in doubt at present.

But it would be misleading to imply that the predominant explicit reason for buying was a shortage of good council housing or the allocation procedures adopted. Most buyers described two main attractions in buying - the first, financial, the second, the belief that it gave security, privacy and independence (Table 4.2). Typical responses about the financial advantages were the following:

'It's a saving in the long run. Renting is dead money.'

'Rents are always going up. You're paying for the rest of your life and it's still not yours. It's an investment to buy.'

'It's cheaper in the long run. I could go on paying rent for ever whereas in eleven years I could cash in my endowment and pay the mortgage off.'

'Renting is a mug's game.'

'We'd be batting our heads against a brick wall by renting. It's dear buying but our own house will be going up in value. We can buy another with a garden later on.'

'It's something to leave for the children.'

'It means your money is growing in value as the house appreciates.'

The fact that many owners saw the house as an investment is particularly interesting in view of the very low levels of house price inflation noted in the previous chapter. It is clear that many buyers had no conception of the long-term relative decline in value to which their dwellings are subject. In part this must be because in general house prices have risen - even if relative values have fallen. In addition, there is a strong ideological bias in our society in favour of holding such a belief. The belief in the investment value of buying is also being strengthened by the existence of rising rents. Most respondents saw paying rent as giving no return. Some, notably the Asians, were consistent in seeing mortgage interest in this light too, and so were reluctant to pay it, but most did not see interest in this way.

Security and independence were the other factors most quoted by buyers. In inner Birmingham 36 per cent and in Anfield 26 per cent of buyers said that the advantages of buying were freedom, privacy and security and the fact that 'it is your own house'. Such views probably have two origins - the first arising from the type of accommodation that the family previously occupied, the second from real and imagined differences in the legal position of owners and renters. Most of the buyers had previously shared their accommodation either with a parent, relative or friend or were in a multi-occupied rented house. Their image of 'continuing to rent' would therefore have been one of continued lack of privacy, landlord or relative interference however well-meaning, and an inability to call a place one's own. The second source of this view lies in the reality of the weak security of tenure enjoyed by council tenants until the 1980 Housing Act. But more generally, many are deterred from renting by the very existence of a landlord at all, with the constant likelihood that any type of issue, such as poor relations with neighbours, will be converted into poor relations with the landlord. It is like the different between being self-employed and having a boss. The first implies greater 'freedom', but greater responsibility and worry. When we asked for their reasons for buying, we saw the owners relishing their freedom. In chapter 6 we will see them struggling with their responsibilities, in terms of repairs and maintenance.

There were notable ethnic differences in the emphasis given to financial as against social and security advantages of buying (Table 4.3). British and Irish buyers tended to emphasise the financial advantages while Asians, and to a less extent West Indians, tended to emphasise security and freedom. Given the evidence we have of racial discrimination in the public and private sectors, this may well reflect their fears of adverse treatment by landlords, both individuals and institutions. Situation testing in the private rental market has tended to reveal higher levels of discrimination than in the owner-occupied market (Smith, 1977).

Other factors affecting Asians, and to a less extent West Indians, relate to the process of migration. For instance, there is often an obligation or desire to offer hospitality to relatives and friends in the process of migration (Dahya, 1974). This may not be possible under rental agreements. There is also the desire to have a secure, rent-free, mortgage-free home in case of unemployment and in some cases the desire for a cashable asset to enable them to have a return visit to their original home or to finance a permanent return. Dahya (1974) adds another factor, that land ownership in Asia is a traditional mark of status and 'izzat' (honour). Such a demonstration of status is all the more important to an emigrant, in order to show success from emigrating. However, home ownership is also a mark of status for white British people, yet this does not mean that everyone strives to own at all costs. We must therefore see 'izzat' as a contributory but not an overriding factor. It may be a diminishing one when weighed against the poor quality of housing so many Asians are buying and the realities of the costs and worries of owning.

Table 4.3
Way in Which Present House Found

	Birmingham (weighted sample)	Birmingham excl. sitting tenants	Liverpool	Liverpool excl. sitting tenants
	%	%	%	%
Advertisement	16	17	19	22
Estate agent	35	37	39	46
Auction	1	2	–	–
Friend	29	30	14	16
Relative	6	5	9	11
Notice in window	6	6	3	4
Bought as sitting tenant	5	–	14	–
Other	3	2	2	2
No reply	–	–	–	–
Total	100	100	100	100
(Weighted) N =	769	722	213	180

Source: Survey.

In general then, though our buyers had broken with the average behaviour pattern of their income group and bought rather than rented, there is little in the attitudinal data to provide support for the view that they regarded owner-occupation as a particularly ideal tenure. Most were buying for pragmatic reasons, notably what they regarded as a financial advantage. If this belief turns out to be based more on the ideology of home ownership (Kemeny, 1981) than on any real advantages of being a low income home-owner in inner Birmingham or Liverpool, the strength of the motivation of these groups and their children towards home ownership is vulnerable to erosion by experience. Again we return to the question of whether these people will persist in owning and whether others like them will continue to follow suit. In particular the Asians, who are dominant amongst inner city buyers in Birmingham, currently stress independence more than financial advantages in their decision to buy. They may therefore be willing to make greater financial sacrifices to continue to do so. In effect, as we stressed earlier, tenure decisions are not just based on conditions or price trends in the owner-occupied sector. What happens to the quantity and quality of rented housing, and to environmental conditions, management styles and rents in the public sector are of crucial importance as push factors. In reality, these buyers are usually trying to find the lesser evil rather than the greatest good.

FINDING A HOUSE

One aspect of buying in inner city areas which remains poorly
understood is the way in which households go about finding a house to
buy. The conventional wisdom is that, because buying a house is the
single largest purchase a person ever makes, buying is likely to be
done with particular care. This should apply, if anything, even more
to lower-income buyers than to those with average or above average
incomes and secure employment. One might therefore expect that
households buying in inner Birmingham and Liverpool would be well
advised to draw heavily on the advice and expertise of specialists in
this field and to shop around, with particular care to compare prices,
quality, location etc. In fact, in many cases the opposite occurred,
and one of the most important findings of the buyers' survey was the
contrast between the outcomes of the transactions which were informal,
almost casual, and the outcomes of transactions where solicitors and
estate agents played a more positive role.

Table 4.3 shows the means through which recent buyers in inner
Birmingham and Liverpool found the home they bought. It is
particularly notable that, even excluding sitting tenants, only a
minority of buyers found their house by using the services of an estate
agent; only just over a third in Birmingham and not quite a half in
Liverpool. The majority of households found their house by one or
other informal means, and this was especially true of Asian buyers
(Table 4.4). Thus, no less than 52 per cent of Pakistani buyers and 39
per cent of Indian buyers found their house through either friends or
relatives. The other point to note is the similarity between British-
born, West Indian and East African Asian buyers in Birmingham and
buyers in Liverpool. Also, even among these groups, the use of estate
agents was much less than might have been expected given the very high
percentage of sales normally made with the services of estate agents.

Another major feature of the search for a house was the remarkably
small number of houses looked at by prospective buyers (see Table 4.5).
Thirty four per cent of buyers in Birmingham (excluding sitting tenant
buyers) and 28 per cent in Liverpool did not look at any house other
than the one they bought. A further 11 per cent in Birmingham and 13
per cent in Liverpool looked at only one other house. Only a small
minority of buyers looked at more than six properties. It is clear
then that many buyers did not 'shop around' comparing prices and
conditions but bought the first or second house they looked at.

As we would expect from the informal way in which they found their
houses, it was the Asians and Irish who were least likely to have
looked at more than one property. In the case of the Pakistanis, this
is mostly related to the fact that the majority of them found their
house through a friend or relation, though there was also a minor
effect of purchases at auctions. However the biggest contrast was
between West Indians and East African Asians on one side and all other
groups on the other. Amongst West Indians and East African Asians, the
largest groups (45 per cent and 54 per cent respectively) had looked at
four or more properties. Amongst East Africans 27 per cent had looked
at over ten properties. If we exclude sitting tenant purchasers the
distinction remains. The most likely reason for the difference between
the West Indians and East Africans as opposed to the other Asian groups

59

probably lies in their much greater command of English, their looser
community ties and, relative to Pakistanis in particular, higher
incomes, and therefore ability to absorb the costs of searching more
widely for better properties. Another factor may of course be greater
competition for the better properties they were attempting to buy. The
poorer Asians buying cheaper older property may have had few
competitors.

Table 4.4
Way in Which Present House Found by Country of Birth

	England Scotland or Wales	Ulster or Eire	Pakistan	India	West Indian	East Africa
	%	%	%	%	%	%
Advertisement	26	22	8	9	32	(27)
Estate agent	37	(37)	28	33	40	(53)
Auction	-	-	3	2	-	-
Friend	9	(18)	44	33	15	(18)
Relative	5	(3)	8	6	2	-
Sitting tenant	18	(10)	1	4	-	-
Notice in window	2	-	6	9	11	(2)
Other	4	(10)	1	4	-	-
Don't know/ no information	-	-	1	*	-	-
Total	100	100	100	100	100	100
Weighted N =	142	36	261	204	62	45

Source: Survey.

Table 4.5
How Many Houses Looked At

How many houses looked at (inc.this one)	Birmingham (weighted sample)		Anfield Liverpool	
	Inc.sitting tenants	Excl.sitting tenants	Inc.sitting tenants	Excl.sitting tenants
	%	%	%	%
One only	38	34	37	28
2	10	11	12	13
3	15	15	13	14
4 - 6	17	18	16	18
7 - 9	7	7	10	12
10 - 13	6	6	4	4
14 or more	5	5	7	9
Indefinite number	3	4	2	2
Total	100	100	100	100
(Weighted) N =	769	722	213	180

Source: Survey.

But what is particularly striking about these findings is the extreme informality of the buying process amongst certain groups, notably the Pakistanis and Indians. Many were treating buying as something you did by contacting a friend who was selling a property or who would suggest one. There was either a mistrust of agents or a feeling that they were not necessary, or perhaps that they were too expensive. By entering the process of buying with this very informal approach, Pakistanis in particular appear to adopt a style of purchase and financial arrangements which is very different from that of the average white or West Indian buyer. In some instances we even had the impression that the idea to purchase was initiated not by the purchaser but by the vendor of a property or a mutual friend or relation of the buyer and seller. Such procedures reduce costs for the vendor but they may create problems for many buyers.

Another striking characteristic of the search for houses is the air of haste about it. More than half the buyers looked at three houses or less. A third looked at only the one they bought. More than half found a house in less than three months from the day they started looking. As we saw earlier, one of the main reasons for not considering council housing was that it was believed to involve too long a wait. This urgency had a marked effect not only upon the care with which houses were selected but also the financial arrangements they were willing to make and their general bargaining position vis-a-vis the vendor. Someone who looks at only one house, does not use the services of estate agents and does not get the house surveyed or valued by a conventional mortgage lender, has no means of telling how its price and condition compare with others on the market. In many instances it appeared that Asian buyers were really relying on the bona fides of the friend or relation who recommended the property to them and that this was more important than 'shopping around'.

Clearly, when a large number of houses are sold in this informal way individual prices will tend not to reflect scarcity, demand or relative values with any consistency. At one extreme, some buyers may purchase just by taking over an existing mortgage, and thus may pay far less than the house is worth. More commonly buyers pay far more than the houses are worth.

Amongst Asians what we may be seeing here is a strategy for avoiding encounters with potentially discriminatory or otherwise unpleasant situations. It has been documented by Fenton (1977) and others that these 'avoiding strategies' are common amongst Asian buyers. They take various forms. One is to buy from and sell to other Asians. Another is not to 'shop around' but to take the first property offered, so that the financial costs of a wide search and the emotional costs of being rejected are avoided. The cost of these strategies is often that buyers have to pay more for the properties they buy (Fenton, 1977; Karn, 1969; Wilkinson and Gulliver, 1971). The fact that West Indians and East African Asians did not generally adopt the same pattern needs to be explained. On the whole, Smith (1977) has found that avoiding strategies and reliance on community contacts are more prevalent amongst those with least command of English, who also coincide with the poorest and often least educated. In our samples, the West Indians and

East African Asians were consistently better off financially than were Indians or, even more so, Pakistanis. The West Indian and East African buyers appeared to be somewhat aspiring, upwardly mobile members of their community, a fact which probably relates to the tendency for the average West Indian to rent a council house; those that buy are seeking something better than a council property. In contrast, national surveys have shown that outside London poorer Asians are the most likely to own a house (Smith, 1977); ownership has been a quick source of relatively cheap shelter.

The informality of the search for the house by many buyers parallels the heavy dependence of buyers on unconventional finance noted in Chapter 3. Indeed, the two processes, the search for the house and the search for finance, both need to be understood in relation to the general approach of the buyers. Amongst immigrants, for instance, it is clear that the housing strategies of West Indians, who have mostly been in this country a considerable time, are significantly different from those of the most recently arrived Pakistanis. The quick and relatively cheap form of minimal shelter which ownership provides for them is far from the conventional image of owner-occupation as the tenure of the most secure and most affluent workers.

5 Negotiating a loan

In Chapter 3 we saw that there were marked contrasts between the financial arrangements made by buyers in Anfield and buyers in inner Birmingham, between those who bought in Anfield's housing action area and the rest of the area and, in particular, between the different areas and ethnic groups in Birmingham (see Tables 3.6, 3.7, 3.8). Are the contrasting patterns to be explained entirely in terms of institutional lenders' differential treatment of different groups or areas or did the groups themselves adopt distinctive borrowing strategies? Or are there elements of both explanations?

Let us begin by asking whether the markedly higher rate of building society lending in Anfield (45 per cent), Sparkhill (45 per cent) and Handsworth (39 per cent), as compared with Soho (12 per cent) and Saltley (8 per cent) can be explained in terms of lower levels of applications for loans (Table 5.1). Did buyers in Birmingham's four areas apply to building societies as often as buyers in Anfield and were they as successful when they applied? It emerged that in Anfield 59 per cent of buyers had had at least one attempt to borrow from a building society during the course of their move to their present house. Normally they were trying to borrow on the house they subsequently bought but in some cases an unsuccessful attempt to buy another house was involved. In Birmingham, the proportion of buyers who had tried to raise a building society loan was much lower, only 37 per cent. However, there were striking differences between the four areas. In Sparkhill 60 per cent had applied to a building society, compared with 51 per cent in Handsworth, 31 per cent in Soho and 19 per cent in Saltley. So the areas with higher lending rates also had larger proportions applying for loans. But were there any differences in the success rates of those who applied? In fact we find (Table 5.1) that not only were people much more likely to apply to building societies in Sparkhill, Handsworth and Anfield but they were also much more likely to be successful when they did. The proportions of successful applicants were as follows: Anfield 76 per cent, Handsworth 76 per cent, Sparkhill 75 per cent, Soho 38 per cent and Saltley 46 per cent.

Next we need to know if the lower success rates were because people had failed to take up building society loans when they were offered or because they were refused a loan. In fact, the lower success rates in Saltley and Soho were associated with an extremely high incidence of refusals. No less than 86 per cent of building society applicants in these two areas had had a refusal at some point, though a proportion of these had persevered with applications and eventually obtained one. But far less of those who had refusals in Saltley and Soho subsequently obtained building society loans; in those two areas only 17 per cent of

Table 5.1
Success Rates for Applicants to Building Societies by Area

	Saltley	Soho	Sparkhill	Handsworth	All 4 B'ham areas	Liverpool Anfield
Percentage of all buyers receiving building society loans	% 8	% 12	% 45	% 39	% 25	% 45
N =	168	170	146	130	769 (weighted)	213
Percentage of all buyers applying to building societies	% 17	% 31	% 60	% 51	% 37	% 59
N =	168	170	146	130	769 (weighted)	213
Percentage of building society applicants receiving building society loan	% (46)	% 38	% 75	% 76	% 67	% 76
N =	28	53	87	66	281 (weighted)	125
Percentage of building society applicants refused at some point	% (86)	% 87	% 32	% 56	% 59	% 49
N =	28	53	87	66	281 (weighted)	125
Percentage of those given a refusal who subsequently obtained a building society loan	% (17)	% (17)	% (46)	% (57)	% 35	% 49
N =	24	46	28	37	166 (weighted)	61

Figures in brackets are based on a total sample of less than 50.
Source: Survey.

those who had had a refusal subsequently obtained a building society loan as compared with 46 per cent in Sparkhill, 49 per cent in Anfield and 57 per cent in Handsworth. (The sample sizes are rather small here but the tendency is consistent with the more reliable data on refusals and successes. See also note to Table 5.2).

When confronted with evidence of low rates of building society lending in the inner city, building societies are apt to respond that these low rates of lending are the result of lack of applications rather than their own unwillingness to lend. Their critics tend to reply that the low level of applications is partly the result of expectations of failure, produced by past building society behaviour. Our results support the latter view. The areas with the lowest building society application rates were those where the building societies' response to applications was exceedingly negative.

There were some other very interesting differences between the areas in terms of the particular societies lending there. Very little has been said before about the impact of variations in lending policies and practices between different building societies and between different branches of the same society (though see Doling and Williams, 1983). Our study, however, points to this as an issue that should be examined closely both by local authorities concerned about the lending situation in inner areas and more importantly by the building societies themselves, who currently do little to monitor the nature of the lending that their branches do and have no mechanism at all for monitoring the lending that they refuse to do. What then were the lending patterns of individual societies in our five areas that led us to be concerned about policies and practices?

In Anfield and Sparkhill the major feature of lending was the dominance of one society in the lending in each area (Table 5.2). In Anfield the 'A'(1) accounted for 35 per cent of all building society lending. There were two other building societies, the 'B' and the 'C' which accounted for 15 per cent and 13 per cent respectively but the rest of the building society lending was evenly spread between a large number of societies each with a few loans. Refusals were roughly proportional to lending except that the 'C' had relatively few refusals. This was because this society had an arrangement with a particular landlord to lend on sales to his sitting tenants.

In Sparkhill the concentration on one society was even more marked. One society, the 'B', accounted for 48 per cent of lending. The next, the 'A', had only 9 per cent. Refusals had a rather different pattern. The 'B' was very under-represented (19 per cent) and the 'A' heavily over-represented (31 per cent), showing that the former was lending far more than the level of applications to it would have led us to expect, while the latter was lending less.

In Handsworth, the other area where the level of building society lending was moderately high, there was, in contrast, no dominant lender. Out of the 48 loans in the sample, one society, the 'A' again, gave 8 loans (17 per cent), another, the 'H', 6 (12 per cent). The other 34 loans were fairly evenly spread between 11 societies. So

Table 5.2
Sources of Building Society Loans by Area.[+]

	Successful Applications	Refused Applications	Successful and Refused Applications
In Anfield	%	%	%
To The 'A'	35	38	36
The 'B'	15	17	16
The 'C'	13	5	9
The 'D'	4	8	6
The 'E'	3	6	4
The 'F'	2	6	4
All others	28	20	25
	100	100	100
* N=	95	65	160
In Sparkhill	%	%	%
To The 'B'	48	(19)	41
The 'A'	9	(31)	16
The 'G'	6	(11)	8
The 'C'	6	–	4
The 'E'	2	(19)	7
The 'H'	3	(11)	6
All others	25	(8)	18
	100	100	100
*. N=	64	26	90
In Handsworth	%	%	%
To The 'A'	(17)	(21)	19
The 'H'	(12)	(8)	10
The 'D'	(10)	(3)	7
The 'I'	(8)	(3)	6
The 'E'	(8)	(5)	7
The 'F'	(8)	(18)	13
The 'B'	(6)	(11)	8
The 'J'	(6)	(3)	5
The 'G'	(6)	(13)	9
The 'K'	(6)	(8)	7
All others	(12)	(7)	9
	100	100	100
* N=	48	38	86

(continued on next page)

Table 5.2 (continued)

In Soho	%	%	%
To The 'I'	(16)	(5)	9
The 'A'	(16)	(3)	7
The 'K'	(11)	(79)	56
The 'G'	(11)	–	4
The 'E'	(11)	–	4
The 'D'	(11)	–	4
The 'B'	(11)	–	4
All others	(13)	(13)	13
	100	100	100
*N=	19	38	57

In Saltley	%	%	%
To The 'B'	(36)	(21)	(28)
The 'C'	–	(21)	(12)
The 'A'	–	(11)	(6)
The 'E'	–	(11)	(6)
The 'H'	–	(11)	(6)
All others	(64)	(25)	(42)
	100	100	100
*N=	14	19	33

Percentage in brackets are based on total samples of less than 50.

* Number of applications to named building societies.

+ In this table the sample sizes become very small. However, it should be remembered that the samples represent every third buyer between 1975 and 1979 in Saltley, Handsworth and Anfield and every second in Sparkhill and Soho (see page 22).

This heavy coverage, along with the systematic sampling method and relative uniformity of stock means that we can be somewhat more confident of our findings within the areas than the sample sizes suggest.

Source: Survey.

unlike Sparkhill and Anfield, Handsworth's fairly favourable lending situation relied on modest levels of lending from a wide range of societies. The 38 refused applications in the area were less evenly spread in that three societies, the 'F', the 'C' and the 'B' accounted for 42 per cent of the refusals but only 20 per cent of the loans.

In Soho, the position was much more extreme. There, one local society, the 'K', accounted for 30 (79 per cent) of the 38 refusals but only 2 (11 per cent) of the 19 loans. The 'I' and the 'A' together accounted for only 8 per cent of the refusals but 32 per cent of the loans. Had the 'K''s ratio of approvals to applications been similar to that of the 'B' in Sparkhill, Soho's lending pattern might have resembled that of Sparkhill. This shows just how important individual societies can be in influencing lending patterns.

Saltley, like Soho, had a very low level of building society lending but also had a lower level of applications and no single society dominated the refusals. The 'B' was again the largest lender giving 5 (36 per cent) of the 14 loans, but no other society gave more than one loan. The 'C' had the worst record, refusing 4 (21 per cent) of the 19 applications and giving none, but the 'B' itself had refused 4 whilst giving 5.

What general points emerged from these patterns? First, though it has been argued that the largest societies are more restrictive in their lending, and small local societies more responsive, this is supported neither by our results nor by those of a CURS Housing Monitoring Team study in Dudley (Housing Monitoring Team, 1982 p. 31). In our areas, two of the largest societies nationally, the A and the B, had overall the largest share of lending. However, two other large ones, the 'E' and the 'H', scarcely featured in the lending and the 'E' had a particularly bad refusal rate in Sparkhill. No local society featured prominently amongst the lenders and one of these, the 'K' had the worst refusal rate of any society in the Birmingham survey areas.

Second, we can see that even though the 'A' and the 'B' had the best record, they were not lending consistently in all areas. This can be explained partly by the presence or absence of branch offices and agencies and by lower application levels but not entirely. Even when applications were being made, the 'B' treated them more favourably in Sparkhill than in any of the other areas. It was unhelpful in Handsworth. The 'A' was particularly helpful in Anfield and Handsworth and remarkably unhelpful in Sparkhill. There are two ways of interpreting these results. One is that particular building societies have different policies towards particular areas or towards house-types or types of borrower which are concentrated in particular areas. The other is that there is a great variety in the mode of operation of different branches. The latter seems by far the most likely explanation and is borne out by the CURS Housing Monitoring Team's study of building societies in Dudley. They analysed the lending of different branches of the same society and concluded that 'the evidence from the survey was that managers did use their discretion... and even though societies might believe that a uniformity of practice was established, in reality variations did occur. Interestingly, branch managers often suggested that what they did was "normal", i.e. the typical practice of all branch managers. Again the survey points out the variations in what is seen as "normal".' (ibid p. 14).

The areas over which branch managers operate discretion depend on the practice of building societies. Branch managers, when questioned about lending decisions, tend to ascribe much responsibility to surveyors, yet the roles of surveyors vary greatly. Some building societies feel that the valuer should only value the property and it is for the society to assess the adequacy of the security offered (Byrom, 1979; p. 103). In other cases, 'although the RICS and other institutions do not give full approval, some valuers will also comment on the percentage advance which should be made and the term of years in quite precise terms... What is clear is that in most cases valuers say nothing about the ratio of earnings to mortgage, the size of the deposit required before consideration, membership terms and other factors and in a large number of cases they say little or nothing about the percentage advance or loan 'term' (ibid: pp. 60-61). So managers have to take a whole range of decisions about lending, from the assessment of the borrowers and property to the terms of the loan. That they do make decisions about property as well as people shows up in our data on the reasons for refusals and the stage at which they occur. It emerged that most of the refused applications to building societies had been refusals made in response to an initial enquiry. The application had not even reached the interview or survey stage. In inner Birmingham and Anfield over 70 per cent of all refusals were at an initial enquiry and less than a quarter reached the property survey stage. Sparkhill was the only area where refusals were given at a later stage and even there 40 per cent of rejections were at initial enquiry (Table 5.3).

Table 5.3
Stage at which Building Society Mortgage Applications were Refused

Refusal stage	Saltley	Soho	Sparkhill	Handsworth	All 4 B'nam areas	Anfield
	%	%	%	%	%	%
On initial enquiry	(80)+	(79)+	(40)+	(76)+	71	72
After interview	(5)	(5)	(24)	(11)	11	6
After property survey	(15)	(16)	(36)	(14)	18	22
Total	100	100	100	100	100	100
(Weighted) N=	20	38	25	37	150	65

Source: Survey.

+ See note to Table 2.5.

There are, of course, many instances when a refusal at initial enquiry is entirely justified, for example, if there is no lending available at the time or if, in turning away a non-saver, the building society is confident that its rule of lending to savers only is not

Table 5.4
Route to Building Society Loans in Anfield and Sparkhill

		Anfield	Sparkhill
1.	Those who obtained building society loan with no apparent agent or solicitor help	%	%
a)	No savings with lender	5	8
b)	With savings with lender	30	41
	Sub Total: Those with no help	35	49
2.	Those who received help in obtaining loan		
a)	Building society loan automatically given with house – organised by vendor or vendor's agent	12	–
b)	Advised by housing assoc. with links with BS	–	1
c)	Building society or insurance co. loan negotiated by solicitor	23	11
d)	Estate agent	15	25
e)	Insurance broker/agent/mortgage broker	3	3
	Sub Total: those with estate agent/solicitor help	53	40
f)	Local authority nominations to building society or and loan by BS and local authority	7	6
g)	Building society loan organised by friend or relation working for or saving with building society	4	4
	Total with any help	64	50
	All with building society loans	100	100
	Number of households	95	65

Source: Survey.

being breached elsewhere. However, to refuse on initial enquiry on the grounds that the area or dwelling type is unsuitable smacks of the 'red-lining' approach which building societies deny exists. We found that over a quarter of the buyers who were refused a building society mortgage at the initial enquiry stage in inner Birmingham and Anfield said the reason given was that the society did not lend in that area, or that they were buying the wrong type or age of property. This tendency to dismiss certain property unseen obviously affects very adversely people buying properties in the poorer areas, which means disproportionately Asians.

This finding, combined with our evidence (despite small samples) of differential success rates of applicants in different areas with the same building society, and the Housing Monitoring Team's (1982) evidence from Dudley of different patterns of lending by different branches of the same building society, points to considerable variation in branch manager practice (see also Doling and Williams, 1983). Our evidence relates most to the ways in which this affects levels of lending and the selection of borrowers. The Housing Monitoring Team's study (1982) which had no access to refusals data was mainly concerned with lending terms but it also considered membership and other access rationing systems. They concluded that 'Managers have the opportunity to vary the membership requirements, size of deposit, ratio of income to advance, loan term, retentions, entry to a pipeline and numerous other factors which go to make up lending practices. Managers were shown to interpret the rules differently and this gives some indication of the very uneven nature of the lending situation in a locality' (ibid p. 63).

Building societies argue that they treat every case on its merits but:

> ...managers like all persons in such a role, have strongly held views about what constitutes a good case, and for that matter, a bad case. In fact such opinions are developed from their own experience as well as the models put forward by their respective societies. This meant that 'each case on its merits' was an overly neutral expression for the reality of the situation. (ibid p. 17).

Without a survey such as ours or extremely close contacts with estate agents, it is impossible for a local authority to know the lending attitudes of a particular building society or one of its branches. There is also no automatic mechanism through which the local authority or another competing building society can be alerted to the existence of mortgage famine created by the unwillingness of a crucial branch to lend in a particular area. This has continued even through the recent period when the societies have been competing for borrowers. From the Housing Monitoring Team research it appears that branch managers are unlikely to have any idea of the impact of their own decisions.

... it was quite clear from the interviews that the branch managers
had little impression of the local market as a whole and no
conception of their significance within it (in terms of what they
did having any effect). The general flavour of the comments was
that the market was something they reacted to and over which they
exercised no control. (ibid p. 21).

Would-be borrowers have little chance of knowing in advance which
societies are most likely to lend to them. As most societies require a
minimum period of saving before an application for a loan will be
accepted, would-be borrowers are committed to a society long before
they approach it about a loan. At this stage they have no real
opportunity to learn anything about different approaches to lending.
Indeed, since much relies on branch manager decisions, it can be argued
that the information they need does not exist. In addition, building
societies tend to stress how normal their procedures are and they
therefore tend to give potential borrowers the impression that all
building societies are relatively alike. On the whole, then, borrowers
will not become aware of a problem until they have actually applied for
a loan and been refused, and then, because of the impression given,
they will tend to believe that all societies would give the same
response. It would be almost unheard of for one society, in refusing a
loan, to suggest to an applicant that he or she tried another. In
these circumstances then, the only way compensatory activity can come
about is if potential borrowers, turned down by one society, are
advised and helped by some agency to find a society that is more
willing to lend. Without such help and advice, potential borrowers
will have no reason to suppose that other societies will have a more
favourable attitude towards them or the property they wish to buy.
They may, as a result, either abandon buying, try a different area or
newer property or borrow from a bank or friends. Given the high
failure rate of mortgage applications in the inner city, the role of
agencies which assist people in the buying process is all the more
crucial.

The remarkable dominance of two building societies in supporting the
level of borrowing in Anfield and Sparkhill obviously warrants further
exploration. Why should buyers in these areas apply so frequently to
these two building societies and why should they be more successful in
their applications to one building society in one area (notably the 'B'
in Sparkhill) than to other building societies in the same area or to
the same building society in a different area? To seek explanations we
examined in detail the processes through which buyers in these two
areas obtained mortgages.

What emerged in both areas was the crucial role played by exchange
professionals, notably the solicitors in Liverpool and the estate
agents in Sparkhill. Those who obtained building society mortgages
without their help were almost entirely first-time buyers who were
long-standing savers with a building society and who successfully
obtained a loan from that society. People who had little or no
building society savings, or had to turn to a society other than the
one they saved with, almost all needed help. To understand a little
more of these cases we will categorise them and give illustrations.
Table 5.4 shows an analysis of the way in which people obtained
building society loans in Anfield and Sparkhill. It shows that only 35

per cent in Anfield and 49 per cent in Sparkhill obtained loans without
help. This does not mean the others would have failed without help. In
Anfield many buyers made no independent advances to a building society
but relied on their agent or solicitor right from the start, whether or
not they would have been successful with the society with which they
saved. In Anfield, for instance, 12 per cent of the buyers found they
automatically obtained a mortgage by purchasing the house; these were
mostly sitting tenants whose landlord or his agent, had made an
arrangement with the 'C' building society to lend on his property when
it passed into owner-occupation. However, these were exceptional. What
usually happened was that the solicitor or estate agent organised the
mortgage, either right from the start or when the client had failed.
Eighty-six per cent in Anfield and 84 per cent in Sparkhill of those
who obtained a building society mortgage independently had savings with
the building society concerned. The comparable figures for those who
got a mortgage via a solicitor or agent were 20 per cent in Anfield and
37 per cent in Sparkhill. Most of the others who needed professional
help had savings with other societies or banks but some for short
periods only. In Sparkhill 14 per cent and in Anfield 13 per cent had
no savings with any society or bank though one invested £100 at his
solicitor's recommendation when the loan request was put in. In
another case, in Sparkhill, the purchaser transferred his building
society account from another society to the one which his agent
represented.

Let us just look at some of the cases in Liverpool and Birmingham:

Mr B: 'The solicitor, insurance company and building society were
all tied up together in the loan from the 'D' Building Society. We
didn't apply to the 'B' because we heard that you needed to have
saved for two years with them and we'd only been with them six
months' (He had saved £500 with the 'B' for 6 months).

Mr C: 'The estate agent suggested trying the 'X' Insurance Company.
We just filled in a form and three weeks later it came through.'
(He had saved £300 over 3 years with a bank).

Mr D: 'We applied to the 'F' but they said they weren't lending any
money till the following March so the estate agent got us one right
away through the 'A'.' (He had saved £2,000 with the 'F' over 7
years).

Mr E: applied to the 'A' with whom he had saved £3,000 over 5
years but was told there was a waiting list and he would have lost
the house by that time. The council was no longer lending in that
area either. However, he eventually received a mortgage from the
'A' via his solicitor. He commented, 'It's funny the 'A' refused
us and then the solicitor got us a loan from the same building
society. Of course, I was giving the solicitor business. You have
to pay them for doing it. Though he was quite cheap.'

Mr F: applied to the 'F' with whom he had saved £1,500 over 2
years. He said they refused because 'they didn't give mortgages out
and haven't done so for 2 years.' He went to his solicitor who
'made a couple of phone calls and got it for me' from the 'L'.

<u>Mr G</u>: 'I really hadn't decided on a house when I first asked the
'E' but in any case they said we weren't earning enough. The age
of the house was all against us too. I think our success had a lot
to do with the estate agent. In fact our deposit wasn't as big as
it should have been' (He was lent £4,559 by the 'B'. Referred by
agent with agency for 'B').

<u>Mr H</u>: 'It was all done for me by the estate agent. It was very
straightforward and there was no problem at all.' (He had no
building society savings, but was lent £5,000 by the 'B').

<u>Mr I</u>: 'We got the mortgage through the agent who said "your age is
right and you're working". He didn't say why some branches of the
building society weren't lending. The agent had to contact several
branches to get this mortgage. He gave £25 to the 'X' branch and
we gave him £50 for himself.' (He was lent £4,925 by the 'B' with
whom he had saved £2,000).

The cases vary in detail but essentially one is seeing the extreme
ease with which solicitors and estate agents with links with certain
building societies could and did arrange mortgages for people in
Anfield and Sparkhill. It is clear why this happens. Building
societies receive investments from and use the professional services of
solicitors (Housing Monitoring Team, 1978). They have agencies with
estate agents and solicitors. They are therefore willing to reserve
loans for solicitors and estate agents even when loans are rationed for
savers. As a bonus for the building society, the borrower may also
become a saver with them in future. The solicitor and estate agent
also benefit. The solicitor will be given, in some cases, the building
society's legal work on the resale of the property, and the agent will
have speeded up the sale of the house and hence the receipt of his
commission.

So if estate agents and solicitors were responsible for the
relatively favourable building society lending patterns in Anfield and
Sparkhill, why did buyers in other areas not have the same level of
help. It is understandable that agents may have had a smaller role,
because of the prevalence of informal sales amongst Asian buyers but
solicitors are involved in every transaction. Why were they so much
more prominent in giving assistance in Anfield's mortgage lending?

Given the fact that Anfield and Sparkhill have many more white buyers
than the other areas, and that white buyers receive more building
society loans than Asians, we have to ask ourselves whether Asian
buyers were receiving less help from agents and solicitors in obtaining
building society loans. An ethnic breakdown of buyers in Sparkhill
according to the way in which they obtained a building society mortgage
suggests (though the sample numbers are rather small) that half the
white building society borrowers and only a third of Asian building
society borrowers received help from an agent or solicitor or from a
friend working for a building society (Table 5.5). These represented
28 per cent of all white buyers but only 15 per cent of Asian buyers.
It was from the differential level of help received from solicitors and
personal contacts that the difference between Asians and whites arose.
There was also a marked difference between Asians and whites who
obtained loans without any help. As well as being far more numerous,

Asians who received no help were also more likely to be saving with the lender (95 per cent of independent borrowers as compared with 67 per cent for white buyers). In other words, Asian and West Indian buyers were more likely to obtain mortgages by the hard route and by meeting all the formal requirements while white buyers more frequently obtained loans without meeting these requirements, through the good offices of an agent or solicitor or even independently. This finding, though based on rather small sample sizes (see note on Table 5.2), confirms the result of an earlier study of race and mortgage lending in Leeds (Stevens et al., 1982).

This is a very serious situation for Asian and West Indian buyers because it means that, effectively, their success rate for mortgage applications is reduced. Table 5.6 shows that refused mortgages represented 39 per cent of effective applications for British and Irish buyers, 33 per cent for East African Asians, 42 per cent for Pakistanis, 53 per cent for Indians and 51 per cent for West Indians. After re-applications the final proportions of successful applicants were 71 per cent for British and Irish, 66 per cent for Pakistanis and Banglaeshi 53 per cent for Indians, 75 per cent for West Indians and 85 per cent for East African Asians. The range between the most and least

Table 5.5
Country of Birth by Route to Building Society Loan - Sparkhill

	British/ Irish	Indian/Pakistani/ East or South African Asian	West Indian
	%	%	No.
1. Building society loan obtained with no apparent help			
a. No savings with lender	(13)	(3)	1
b. Savings with lender	(25)	(58)	-
Sub Total: with no help	(38)	(61)	1
2. Building society loan negotiated by			
a. Solicitor	(16)	(8)	-
b. Estate agent	(25)	(22)	2
c. Insurance agent/broker	(3)	(3)	-
d. Friend or relation working for building society	(6)	-	-
Sub Total: Those with agency help	(50)	(33)	2
e. Friend acted as guarantor	-	(3)	-
f. Help from housing assoc.	(3)	-	-
g. Local authority nominations to building society	(9)	(3)	-
Total with private agency help as per cent of all buyers	28	15	
N=	32	36	3

Source: Survey.

( ) see note to Table 2.5.

Table 5.6
Success Rate of Applicants to Building Societies by Country of Birth:
Birmingham

	British Irish	Pakistani Bangladeshi	Indian	West Indian	E.African Asian
Applicants successful (per cent)	71	(66)	53	(75)	(85)
No. of applicants N=	90	32	79	40	33
Applications refused (per cent)	39	(42)	53	51	(33)
Total No. of effective applications+ N=	105	36	89	61	42

+ This includes all previous applications to a building society
whether or not they were successful. It excludes applications which
fell through for reasons other than a rejection by the building
society e.g. the property being sold to another buyer.

Source: Survey.

successful was therefore 32 per cent. It could be argued that what we
are seeing here is the effect of incomes rather than anything to do
with race. This could certainly explain the high success rates of the
West Indians and East African Asians, two groups with relatively good
income levels. However, it does not explain the very bad position of
the Indians. Also, when we analyse, by income, success rates of
applicants for building society loans, we find that in Birmingham the
variation in success between those with the highest and lowest incomes
was only 10 per cent, that is the difference between 73 per cent and 63
per cent (Table 5.7). In Anfield success rates of building society
applicants were over 10 per cent higher than in Birmingham in each
income band, except the £71 to £80 band in which a large group of
Liverpool buyers obtained local authority loans.

The impact of building society refusals in Birmingham was
particularly harsh in certain areas, notably Soho where many Indians
saved with one local building society (the 'K') which lent very little
in that area. In Sparkhill many Asians obtained mortgages by direct
application because they were saving with building societies that were
lending, notably the 'B'. Those who saved with the 'K' building
society's branch in Soho found themselves in a very different position.
Without help, these savers could not obtain building society loans.
Instead they turned to short term bank loans. Table 5.8 shows that
only 21 per cent of Indians and 12 per cent of Pakistanis who had
previously and unsuccessfully tried to obtain a building society loan
eventually obtained one from another or the same society. This
compares with 46 per cent of British and Irish buyers, 63 per cent of
East African Asians and 50 per cent of West Indians. Here we are
seeing the deterrent effect of rejections on two communities, the

Indians and Pakistanis, who already have a disproportionately small share of building society lending.

We still have to ask ourselves why Indian and Pakistani buyers less often get help from solicitors or personal contacts in obtaining building society loans. There are likely to be a number of reasons. First, in the Asian community there is an extensive network of agents referring potential borrowers to the clearing banks. When an Asian is refused a building society loan, he is likely to turn to this well-established and well-known system. The building societies are now establishing their own network of Asian agents and this may change the picture somewhat. Second, British buyers, perhaps being more aware of the inconsistencies of building society lending may be less willing to take 'no' for an answer. Third, a solicitor's or agent's expectation that an Asian will be willing to turn to a bank for a short-term loan may well affect the situation.

For most purchasers the failure to find a conventional mortgage means that the sale falls through. Therefore estate agents and solicitors whose fees are dependent upon a successful outcome are motivated to help. But for Indians and Pakistanis this appears to be less often the case. When refused by a building society they often turn to loans from banks and from family and friends. If the client is willing to shoulder the very heavy monthly payments involved, the agent and solicitor have little motive for persuading him against such a solution. Asians are therefore in a vicious circle. They are

Table 5.7

Success Rate of Applicants to Building Societies by Income of Head of Household

Weekly net income of head of household	No. of applicants (weighted N)	Per cent of applicants successful	No. of applicants	Per cent of applicants successful
£		%		%
Up to 50	39	(64)	16	(75)
51 - 60	44	(63)	8	(75)
61 - 70	71	65	11	(82)
71 - 80	53	70	23	(56)
81 - 90	34	(73)	17	(88)
91 +	30	(73)	33	(88)

( ) see note to Table 2.5.
Source: Survey.

Table 5.8
Final Source of Finance for Those with Previously Unsuccessful
Applications to Building Societies by Country of Birth: Birmingham

Source of finance	British and Irish	Pakistani	Indian	West Indian	East African Asians
	%	%	%	%	%
Building society	(46)	(12)	(21)	(50)	(63)
Local authority	(31)	–	(12)	(34)	(8)
Bank	(5)	(62)	(40)	(12)	(8)
Finance co., money lender	(3)	–	(6)	–	–
Friends/relations	(3)	(27)	(11)	–	–
Solicitor, estate agent vendor, etc.	–	–	(5)	–	–
Cash	(12)	–	(4)	–	(21)
No reply	–	–	–	(4)	–
Total	100	100	100	100	100
Weighted N=	49	13	47	25	12

( ) see note to Table 2.5.
Source: Survey.

frequently refused conventional mortgages but their willingness to
accept short term loans takes the pressure off solicitors and estate
agents to organise conventional loans for them. It becomes a matter of
'common knowledge' that Asians prefer such loans and have ready access
to large amounts of cash. This stereotype is currently acting to the
disservice of Indians in particular who are making great efforts to
obtain building society loans with little success. Their experience
means that other Indians and Pakistanis are being deterred from
applying at all.

Finally, there is, of course the possibility of direct racial
discrimination. To study this, Political and Economic Planning (PEP)
carried out situation testing on homeowners' contacts with estate
agents. In 1967, it was found that, in contacts with estate agents
about house purchase, West Indians were discriminated against in 64 per
cent of the tests (Daniel, 1968: p. 171). In a third of these
discriminatory situations, it was the availability of mortgages which
was the subject of the discrimination. In another third there was
'steering', that is, a different list of addresses of properties for
sale or no address at all was offered to the West Indian. A repeat of
the tests in 1973, after the 1968 Race Relations Act had been in force
five years, showed a marked drop in this type of discriminatory
behaviour by agents (Smith, 1977: p. 287). In 1973, in 12 per cent of
cases the West Indian or Asian testers were given inferior treatment
and 17 per cent were given different treatment, 29 per cent in all.
This is roughly the same level as that found in the USA in similar
tests (Wienk et al., 1979), not an encouraging comparison given the
extreme racial and social segregation of the US housing market. In

addition, as Wienk points out, the effect is cumulative. 'If 15 per cent of agents discriminate, then a black who visits four sales agents can expect to encounter one or more instances of discrimination 48 per cent of the time' (Wienk et al., 1979: Part E, Section 5, p. 2). The procedures for buying a house are long and complex and only the initial stages of the transaction were being tested, namely approaches to an agent. It is entirely possible that some solicitors adopt the same approach, perhaps through fear that, in being 'swamped' with Asian clients if they appear too helpful, they may become unattractive to white clients and white institutions.

So far we have considered aggregated findings but a case-by-case examination of the processes of purchase and fund-raising provides considerable additional insight into the working of the owner-occupied housing market at its lower price level. So in the last part of this chapter, we will illustrate with individual cases a series of features of the market which have had a very marked effect on the process of buying. The cases help us to understand the patterns already shown in more quantitative form and the individual circumstances and behaviour underlying the statistics.

First, it is important to emphasise that the people concerned were very 'housing hungry'. In our Birmingham survey 73 per cent and, in Anfield, 84 per cent were first time buyers and few had a self-contained home of their own before buying. The vast majority were living with friends and relatives or to a far smaller extent with parents. Yet the majority already had children. They therefore felt considerable pressure to find a property fast. Unlike young couples who share with parents, those who were sharing with other relatives or friends (and these were the vast majority) were often sharing with a family which was itself expanding. This urgency to find a home, it becomes apparent, was often coupled with a belief that the competition for owner-occupied property in the inner city was fierce. It is difficult to tell how realistic this view was. It was certainly true that some had lost property to other buyers, but this is to be expected in any group of buyers. Other evidence suggests that vacancy rates are higher in the inner city housing stock than elsewhere, but this may not necessarily apply to the owner-occupied stock (Bell, 1976).

Whether or not competition was in fact very strong, the belief that it was had a very marked effect upon buyer's behaviour. As an example let us look at the case of Mr J.

Mr J had previously lived with his son in Saltley but this house was being demolished. Mr J heard that another house in Saltley was for sale for £4,500. He was told that if he could raise that sum within 24 hours, he could buy the house. So he rang friends and raised £4,500 in twelve hours, from ten friends, in sums ranging from £100 to £1,000. He also bought the freehold for £550. As soon as the compensation for Mr J's son's previous house, (£3,150) came through, they paid off most of the loans, leaving £1,350 worth of loans still outstanding. These loans were informal but for not more than 18 months. Mr J then applied to the council for £1,350 to replace these informal loans but the council refused saying

that he was not a first time buyer and also was just re-mortgaging the house. He argued that the house was in his own name, not that of his son, who was the owner of the previous house.

This is a clear example of the pressure that buyers feel to raise money quickly. It also demonstrates what has been discussed earlier, namely the ability of Asians to raise money from friends and relations. Asked whether there were any people who find it particularly difficult to obtain a mortgage, one Asian buyer said that it was 'the people who don't share their problems; the people who live for themselves and don't help each other. If you haven't ever helped others with loans they will not help you.' The case also demonstrates the inflexibility and unsuitability for inner city buyers of having local authority lending restricted to first time buyers. There are many inner city second time buyers who are unable to raise conventional loans in any other way. As we have see earlier (Table 2.5), it is Asians who are most likely to be second time buyers in inner Birmingham and therefore appear to be most adversely affected by this rule. However, white and West Indian potential second time buyers may well be more deterred by lack of local authority lending and therefore even more affected.

In the case of Mr K, urgency about buying and fear of losing the property to a rival buyer were combined with anxiety about the length of time that a corporation mortgage would take to arrange. This, along with the unwillingness of building societies to help, led him to take on a short-term loan which he had problems repaying.

Mr K, a Pakistani, bought a house in Sparkhill in August 1977, for £4000. He raised £2000 as a loan from a friend and added to it £2000 of savings. This loan was interest free and the amount paid back monthly varied. Mr K, had six children and he said his friend 'didn't worry him too much' about the repayments because Mr K had so many children to support. However his monthly repayments were still between £70 and £100 depending on his circumstances that month. At the time of the interview he was having difficulty finding the repayments. Similarly repairs and improvements were having to wait; for instance, they had no hot water because the geyser was too small but he could not afford to replace it. Previously he had applied to the 'A' Building Society for a loan of £2000 for the same house but he had been refused on initial enquiry. The reason he said he was given was that they did not lend small amounts. At the time he had been saving nine or ten months with that society and had accumulated £600 to £700. After his refusal he had sent his nephew along to see the council but they had said that a loan would take six months or so. He had already been looking for a house for six months and had seen about 35 houses already. They had either been too expensive or had lacked a bathroom so he did not want to lose this property. His wife was arriving from Pakistan with his children so he decided the only thing to do was to raise a private loan.

The sense of urgency that buyers felt about raising loans fast was, as we saw in the case of Mr J, often produced by the vendors or more usually their agents. Those who are used to the British system of buying and selling houses know that agents invariably claim that there is at least one other potential buyer. But buyers are also aware that unless, and most unusually, the rival has cash, then he too will have delays caused by raising a mortgage or completing the sale of his previous house. A suburban potential buyer, told that he must raise the money in 24 hours if he wished to obtain the house, would almost invariably completely lose interest and look for another property. Most inner city buyers in Birmingham are not only first generation buyers. They are also first generation immigrants into Britain. Their familiarity with the English housing market's bargaining language is therefore minimal.

A factor which clearly complicates all this is the prevalence of short term bank loans as a source of finance for house purchase in the inner city. Because they are not long term loans secured on the property, the processes of lending are much quicker. This means that anyone who is buying with a bank loan can complete the transaction much faster than someone buying with a building society or local authority loan. If these two potential buyers are competing for the same house, the one with the bank loan will get it. The effects of this must be quite critical in the inner city. First, there is an incentive to get a bank loan rather than a conventional loan, especially in areas like Saltley where bank lending is so dominant. Second, because Asians tend to be more willing than other groups to accept bank loans they will be able to compete for properties more effectively. It is a common belief amongst whites in these areas that 'you can't compete with Asians because they have the cash'. Third, use of short term bank loans is even more likely to occur because of the high failure rate of Asians who apply for building society loans.

It is therefore perfectly conceivable that the virtual absence of white or West Indian buyers in certain parts of the market is produced as much by the pattern of institutional lending as it is by ethnic preferences. It appears to be no accident that Soho, which suffered from such a high rate of building society refusals, had scarcely any white buyers at all and very few West Indians between 1975 and 1979. Where West Indians, East Africans and whites are deterred from buying by lack of building society mortgages, Indians and Pakistanis are not.

Faced with all these additional complications, on top of all the usual problems of house purchase, inner city buyers clearly need professional advice and assistance. But it is all too apparent that they find it very difficult to obtain advice that they can trust to be impartial and consistent and which has their interests at heart. The local authority is regarded by most as just another lender like the building societies. One buyer for instance described the local authority as having the 'same regulations and attitudes as the 'H' Building Society'. The 'H' Building Society had refused him a mortgage saying they would lend only on freehold property in good condition or leasehold with over 30 years left at the end of the loan. Another buyer said the local authority 'would not lend on older property' which is why he had not approached them. At that time Birmingham City lent only on pre-1919 property. More generally the local authority was seen, unfortunately justifiably, as just another lender rather than a more general source of advice on buying problems. Very often the people turned for help to friends or acquaintances. This sometimes led to poor advice and made them vulnerable to middle-men seeking a 'cut' on a referral to a bank. As Mr S, an Asian accountant remarked, 'Factory workers find it hard to get mortgages because they don't get good advice. They approach friends and relatives who do their best but don't know the best way and sometimes cheat.'

The building societies, while seen as helpful by the minority funded by them, were a source of exasperation for many of the others. The reasons given for refusing a mortgage often implied a total rejection of lending on inner city older houses or seemed so petty or even ridiculous that they appeared to be excuses for not lending. Usually no advice was offered to unsuccessful applicants about what they should do next. This all happened whilst many applicants had followed all the advice about saving substantially and steadily with a building society. As a result many Asian buyers in particular, but all buyers to some extent, turned away from building societies to the clearing banks who seemed to show in some respects more flexibility in approaching the funding of inner city property. For many Asians too, shorter term loans offered by banks were actually preferred to conventional mortgages. However this was not universally the case and many found difficulties in meeting the higher repayments involved in short term loans and would have preferred a longer loan. It will be interesting to see whether the recent short-lived movement of banks into conventional mortgage lending applied to the inner cities as well as the suburbs, or whether bank lending in these areas remained as in the previous period of active bank lending short-term, higher interest lending. The evidence so far is that recent bank mortgage lending has been concentrated on the more expensive end of the market.

In the following examples of rejected mortgage applications to building societies, we are of course giving only the buyers' interpretation of events but it is, after all, their interpretation which guides their future actions. Examples of applicants to building societies being told that the society did not lend on property 'of that age' or 'in that area' were numerous.

For instance, Mr L borrowed from the 'B' Society to buy a house in the southern end of Sparkhill, in the newest pre-1919 stock in our Birmingham surveys. He had previously been refused a loan by the 'E' Society, with whom he was saving, on the grounds that the house was 'too old'. He obtained the loan from the 'B' because the estate agent involved in selling the house was an agent for that society. The loan was then 'very, very quick indeed'. In this case, the situation was rescued for Mr L by his good fortune in having an estate agent who was also an agent for the 'B'.

Mr M, a Pakistani, was not so fortunate. He had saved £3,000 over three years with the 'K', a local building society, and applied for a £4,000 loan to buy a £6,600 house in Soho. He was told the house was too old. Receiving no further advice he eventually resorted to a one year loan of £2,000 from a friend and a six year loan of £3,000 from an Asian bank. It is clear that Mr M and his friends would gather from this experience that the 'K' Building Society was not interested in older property.

In fact the effect of such experiences on other applicants is well demonstrated in the case of Mr N, an Indian buyer.

Mr N had been a saver with the 'K' Building Society for eight years but when he wanted to buy a house he did not even approach them for a loan, 'because I already knew they did not lend on older houses'. He had tried another building society and the council but the former refused and the latter required £2,000 worth of repairs because of a defect in the rear wall. When he finally managed to buy, instead of trying a building society or the council again, he found a cheaper house at only £3,500 and went straight to an insurance broker for £1,000 which he added to his £2,500 savings. It should be remembered that his unsuccessful approaches to the council and the building society had already cost him survey fees. This example shows that decisions to use short term financing for house purchase can be the reason why cheap property is purchased by Asians, just as much as the purchase of cheap property can be the reason why other forms of loans are not open to them. There is no clear single direction of cause and effect.

Building societies frequently maintain that their poor lending record in inner cities is because people do not apply for mortgages. It is certainly the case that many people fail to apply but it is also clear that the lack of success experienced by many applicants to building societies not only has an effect on their own subsequent behaviour but also creates a more general expectation of failure amongst purchasers in inner cities. Given the close informal contacts between these low income buyers and their heavy reliance on informal buying and selling, it is not surprising that news of this type spreads rapidly and that low expectations of building societies become common knowledge, as do higher expectations of banks.

The building societies themselves therefore help to create the climate in which people fail to apply for their mortgages. This is produced not only by the actual refusal but also by the manner of their refusal to many applicants. In some cases the reasons offered seemed arbitrary or trivial. In less than a quarter of the cases was any advice at all given about how the applicant could be more successful another time. The most usual advice was to wait and come back to the same society when funds were available. As we have seen from the success that buyers who went through agents and solicitors had in obtaining loans from societies, this may not be at all the best strategy. The next most common advice was to try a different property or a different area. Advice to go to the local authority was less often given, but most uncommon was advice to go to another building society. This advice was only offered to three buyers, all of them black. Altogether the impression the societies give to the unsuccessful is not helpful. A few examples will illustrate this.

In 1977 Mr O, a West Indian, was refused a loan by the 'A' Building Society with whom he saved on the grounds that his house in Sparkhill was, at £6,000, overpriced. He then went to the 'B' who agreed to the price and the loan of £5,000 he requested.

Mr P, an Indian, was refused a loan by the 'L' Building Society with whom he had saved for six years. The reason given was that the house had only a 24 year lease when their minimum requirement was 25 years. No suggestion was made, however, that he should negotiate to purchase the freehold along with the leasehold.

The difference in the attitudes of banks comes out in the following case.

> Mr Q had applied for a £2,000 loan on a £3,000 house from the 'K' Building Society with whom he had saved £2,500 over 6 years. He was refused on the grounds that the house was too old and that there was only 18 years on the lease. There was no discussion about the purchase of the freehold. So instead he turned to a clearing bank who lent him £1,800 for the house purchase, £650 to buy the freehold and £400 for repairs. These loans were for four years only and involved him in gross monthly repayments of about £100 a month.

One reason for refusal which was not understood by buyers was that the loan requested was too small (see also McIntosh, 1978). For building societies small loans are associated with cheap houses, regarded as bad risks. In addition fewer large loans obviously involve less administrative costs than more smaller ones. But this means tht purchasers of the lowest priced houses are at a disadvantage, especially if they have saved up substantial deposits in order to reduce the size of the loan and hence the monthly repayments that they need to take on. In this respect, Asian buyers are likely to be most affected since they try to minimise the loans they take out. Banks, too, in their advertisements for normal mortgage lending, tend to include a clause about a minimum loan, typically of £5,000.

The building societies justify rules about minimum loans on grounds not only of administrative costs to themselves but also of the ratio of the survey, legal and administrative costs to the amount borrowed. Despite higher interest and shorter loan periods and hence higher monthly repayments, a bank loan may be the cheaper method of borrowing small sums of money. This should, however, be explained to applicants, instead of them being presented with a bald refusal.

Many applicants were also refused because they were said not to have been saving long enough with a society. This is one of the standard rationing procedures of building societies. The objection that one can make to it is that there is in fact, as we have seen earlier, much lending to non-savers. In addition, long-term savers were often refused. In some cases the savers had more money saved with the building society than the amount they were asking for. The impression remains that building societies are very unenthusiastic about inner city lending and that if applicants are non-savers this is a convenient reason for refusing a mortgage. If they are savers, then refusal has to be on grounds of the age or condition of the property, or that its price is too high or the loan too small. Without the expert help and special pressures that solicitors and estate agents are able to bring to bear upon building societies, individual buyers can only accept these refusals at face value (Housing Monitoring Team 1982; Stevens et.al, 1982).

The low levels of building society lending in inner areas, particularly the Asian areas of Birmingham, appear to arise from an amalgam of factors which are so inter-related that it is impossible to separate one from the other. There is, first, the reluctance of building societies to lend in older inner city areas because of short leases, old property, poor state of repair and cramped physical environment. Added to this are their attitudes towards the social characteristics of the areas, notably their class and race composition, but also the fear of crime, vandalism, etc. In this already complex picture have to be included attitudes, not just to mixed areas but to the ethnic minority applicants themselves. A study in Leeds (Stevens et al, 1982) which controlled for house type showed that both mixed areas and black applicants received less favourable treatment from lenders. The more favourable lending picture in Liverpool where the property was inferior to that in inner Birmingham but the buyers white and slightly better off financially, seems to suggest that buyers are more crucial to lenders than the property is, despite lenders protestations to the contrary.

Then, to make things even more complicated, there is the fact that fewer Asians, especially Pakistanis, apply for conventional loans. This appears to be partly because they are deterred by the prospect of failure, partly because a middle-man system links them with the banks, partly because they are buying housing cheap enough to be financed in this way and partly because they prefer short term loans to minimise interest payments and to allow them to become outright owners as rapidly as possible. So even on this last point it is not possible to distinguish between choice and constraint. Even less on the preceding points about lenders' attitudes is it in any real sense possible to separate out the causal factors since the lenders themselves do not distinguish between them. In this respect discriminatory practices of building societies closely resemble the type of discrimination happening in local authority housing allocations (Karn, 1983). In fact, the whole process of discrimination against areas and against ethnic groups tends to arise at a day to day level of informal decisions. This allows the building societies to believe that because there may be no overt intention to discriminate no such discrimination exists. It also means that for black buyers and for the Commission for Racial Equality it is very difficult to prove discrimination in the case of any one individual buyer. Though evidence has been building up since the early 1970s about racial inequalities in lending (Bassett and Short, 1980b; Boddy, 1976; Burney, 1967; Fenton, 1977; Harrison and Stevens, 1982; Karn, 1977/8; Smith, 1977), the building societies have consistently denied the need for examination of their practices and continue to maintain that the fact that 'every case is taken on its merits' is an adequate safeguard to borrowers. Our survey therefore yet again shows up the need for a much more questioning approach by the building societies and indeed estate agents and solicitors about the effects of their practices on inner areas and minority groups. Greater accountability and openness are needed to achieve a fairer system.

The extreme vulnerability of low income buyers in inner city areas has emerged as a major issue in the American context in the wake of a number of disastrously unsuccessful federal low-income home ownership 'programs'. During House of Representative Hearings on these 'programs', Representative Wednall said (US Congress, 1971: 3):

'While much attention has recently been focussed on the area of consumer protection in the borrowing of money and the purchase of retail goods, little or no attention has been paid to the need for consumer protection in house buying. I think it is safe to say that few home buyers enter the housing market on an equal bargaining position with those selling the house, be it used or new. If the consumer's interest is in general absent from the home-buying field, it is particularly absent from the FHA - subsidised home-buyer program .. in most instances these buyers are people who have had no previous exposure to the phenomenon of home-ownership and all the problems and responsibilities that go with it .. This program has injected into a complex market an extremely unsophisticated buyer and HUD owes a special duty to see that he is fairly treated.'

These comments might equally well be applied to many of the families buying deteriorated housing in inner Birmingham and Liverpool and to the responsibilities of the British government. Though Britain has no equivalent of the HUD programs, current policies are directed towards trying to induce people to buy rather than rent. These policies involve financial incentives to buy, increases in local authority rents and cuts in subsidies for the management and maintenance of council housing. If we are to have such policies, they also carry with them responsibilities towards the people who have been encouraged to buy.

Conclusions

Chapters 4 and 5 have examined the buying process in order to shed light on the inner city housing market structure. A number of distinctive characteristics emerge. In the first place, it is clear that the households who eventually buy in this market are very restricted in the type of housing to which they can gain access. A high percentage are first time buyers, many have large families and have previously been sharing housing with very poor amenities. The almost complete absence of cheap and adequate private rented housing, together with the very long waiting times for good council housing, combine to attract whole groups of households towards the bottom of the owner-occupied housing market. They enter the market with limited resources and with considerable pressure to obtain housing quickly. In short, they are very 'housing hungry'.

In addition, the households often possess inadequate or sometimes misleading information about the possibilities of obtaining finance, about how the complex buying process operates, and about the various alternatives open to them. They tend to rely on friends and relatives and to do little 'shopping around' for houses or finance. This, together with their high and inelastic demand for housing, places pressure on households to buy quickly. On top of this, the widespread belief that the market is very competitive has important consequences for the manner in which purchases are made.

Some of the reasons for the low level of conventional lending in these areas are therefore related to the market condition of the buyers: their urgent need for housing, their limited resources, their lack of expertise and the real or perceived competition for housing. Thus, for example, the need to settle the purchase at great speed deters many buyers from using building society finance and encourages them to take out a personal bank loan. However, it is clear that many of the perceptions of buyers about the reluctance of building societies to lend in the areas studied derive from their own experiences and those of friends and relatives. Some branch managers of building societies are willing to lend but others are not, and this clearly affects the volume of lending in particular areas. In general, there is a reluctance to lend on much of the older property, and if specific building society branches do not engage in deliberate red-lining, then the practical consequences of their actions and procedures are scarcely distinguishable from red-lining.

The overall nature of the inner city housing market is therefore very distinctive. The informal market structure results in a highly personalised transfer system in which information is available in the form of heresay, gossip and anecdotes obtained from friends and relatives. The widespread absence of formal processes means that a market which is sensitive to demand and supply cannot fully emerge. One result of this is that house prices often bear only the most general relationship to those which might be expected from market processes. This is not to deny that market processes operate. Rather, it means that a large proportion of houses will be either overpriced or underpriced relative to the average and that house prices will fluctuate wildly about the mean.

Furthermore, all the evidence suggests that the informality and haphazard market organisation is more marked among the buyers of houses at the very bottom of the inner city market. Just as the market in Birmingham is differentiating into higher priced houses financed with mortgages and bought by British-born and West Indian buyers and lower priced houses bought with informal loans by Asians, so the dependence upon friends and relatives for housing market information, and the consequent absence of professional advice is more widespread among Asians than among other ethnic groups. The overall picture is therefore consistent in all major respects. Increasingly in these inner city areas a bottom strata of housing is emerging - a 'sump' - characterised by the poorest and worst housed buyers, lacking access to market information, buying the first house which a friend or relative suggests and using informal loans.

The concentration of these low income households in such housing has potentially very serious consequences for the expansion of this sump of housing. The clear reluctance of many conventional mortgage lenders to finance the purchase of these houses and their rapidly falling relative value suggests that these low income households are buying houses which are at best a dubious investment. The material condition of this stock of housing is therefore in serious danger of deteriorating very rapidly. In the next chapter we will examine the condition of this housing and examine the viability of the stock in the light of the findings of this and the previous chapter.

NOTES

(1) The Department of Environment requested that no building society should be named in this publication. The alphabetical codes used bear no relation to the initial letters of the societies to which they are applied.

6 Coping with disrepair

The condition of the inner city housing stock was one of the major areas of investigation of the project. A considerable amount of data on house condition which was collected in the recent buyers surveys and the re-interview survey, particularly on the amount of repair and maintenance work carried out by households, and the extent to which they used improvement grants. In addition a special house condition survey of one in five of the properties included in all four Birmingham survey areas was carried out.

The discussion of house condition in this chapter is in two parts. In the first part, the data from the recent buyers and the reinterview surveys are examined to shed light on the repairs and maintenance activity of both recent[1] and longer-established[2] buyers. This part will include discussion of the use of improvement grants. In the second part, the results of the Birmingham house condition survey will be presented.

It has already been noted in Chapter 2 that 10 per cent of houses bought by recent buyers in inner Birmingham lacked a bath or shower. Although this was more than double the percentage in Birmingham as a whole in 1977, it was considerably lower than in Anfield, Liverpool, where around a third of dwellings bought between 1975 and 1979 lacked a bath or shower. This clearly suggests that the houses bought in Anfield were of a considerably lower standard than those bought in the Birmingham areas. However, because we did not have the resources for a house condition survey in Anfield, a comparison between Birmingham and Anfield on the condition of the fabric is not possible from our data. Opinion data from the household surveys is not adequate for this purpose because buyers' judgements as to whether the house needs a new roof or window frames replaced vary and are unrealiable guides to house condition. Nevertheless, an indication as to the kinds of repair work carried out by buyers is at least a minimum measure of the households' perceptions of house condition, although it has to be remembered that many households are unable to afford the repairs that they believe necessary.

Table 6.1 shows the percentage of recent buyers in Birmingham and Anfield who had carried out repair work on various aspects of their houses since buying. It can be seen that up to a quarter of households in the four survey areas in Birmingham and up to 55 per cent of households in Anfield had carried out repair or improvement work on at least one item. The level of work was clearly higher among Anfield buyers – for most items twice as many Anfield buyers as Birmingham buyers had carried out work. Table 6.1 also shows the percentage of

Table 6.1
Improvements Carried out by Buyers in Inner Birmingham and Liverpool
(1979 Buyers Survey)

Improvement or repair carried out	Inner Birmingham			Liverpool: Anfield		
	Households		of which per cent using grant	Households		of which per cent using grant
	No.	%		No.	%	
	No.	%	%	No.	%	%
replastering	189	25	12	118	55	11
rewiring	175	23	13	97	46	13
window frames	164	21	14	88	41	16
guttering	158	20	13	83	39	16
re-roofing	137	18	15	67	32	21
re-pointing	113	15	19	89	42	14
new floors	111	14	14	55	26	26
wood treatment	104	14	12	41	19	20
damp proofing	84	11	17	88	41	16
new chimney	76	10	22	32	15	25
bath/shower	67	9	22	50	24	30
hand wash basin	54	7	28	48	23	31
inside toilet	51	7	31	52	24	29
central heating	42	5	7	17	8	0

Source: Survey.

buyers who used improvement grants when carrying out specific repairs or improvements. In all, 7.2 per cent of Birmingham buyers and 10.8 per cent of Liverpool buyers carried out repairs or improvements with the aid of an improvement grant.

The level of repairs carried out by recent buyers can be compared with that of longer-established buyers in Birmingham, on whom additional data was collected in the re-interview survey (see Table 6.2). It can be seen that, as expected, in inner Birmingham longer-established buyers had in general carried out more repair and improvement work than had recent buyers. Thus, for example, 17 per cent of longer-established buyers had installed an inside toilet compared with 7 per cent of recent buyers; 21 per cent had installed a bath or shower, compared with 9 per cent of recent buyers, while 36 per cent of longer-established buyers had carried out re-roofing, compared with 18 per cent of recent buyers. In all, 84 per cent of longer-established buyers had carried out some repair work. Table 6.2 also shows the proportion of longer term buyers who had particular items of work specified by the lender. It is common for lenders to make a mortgage conditional on certain repairs being carried out. However, remakably few of the repairs carried out by the buyers in our surveys had been specified by the lender, especially in Birmingham, where conventional lending was less frequent than in Liverpool. Even conventional lenders had not, often made repairs stipulations. In Birmingham, the repairs most often specified for recent buyers were rewiring (8 per cent) followed by re-roofing (5 per cent) and damp proofing (7 per cent). In Liverpool, lender specifications were more common. Thus, 24 per cent of buyers carried out damp proofing and 16 per repointing following specification by the lenders.

The other major issues which the surveys addressed were the level of expenditure on repairs and maintenance and the size of improvement grants. Care must be taken with these figures since they span a number of years and so include expenditure on repairs in early years which would cost much more to carry out by the end of the survey period. However, they do provide us with a crude measure of the level of expenditure and in addition indicate the relative amount of money coming from improvement grants and other sources. Table 6.3 shows, in crude aggregate terms, the total amount spent on repairs and maintenance and how much of this came from improvement grants, loans and savings. It can be seen that the total amount spent per household by recent buyers in Liverpool (£1,253) was more than double that spent by recent buyers in Birmingham (£577) and not very much less than that spent by longer-established Birmingham buyers (£1,435). It can also be seen that grants accounted for one-fifth of all expenditure among longer-established buyers and among recent buyers in Liverpool, compared with under one-seventh among recent buyers in Birmingham. The bulk of expenditure came from personal household savings with the

Table 6.2
Improvements Carried out by Longer-Established Buyers in Inner
Birmingham
(re-interview survey)

Improvements carried out	% of house-holds who undertook specified improvements	% of house-holds who had specified improvements required by lender
	%	%
bath/shower	21	1
inside toilet	17	1
wash basin	21	1
other plumbing	23	8
central heating	7	–
double glazing	2	–
rewiring	32	3
re-roofing/ re-tiling	36	2
rebuild chimneys	23	1
repointing	22	2
damp proof course	10	–
new flooring	23	2
woodwork treatment	9	1
replace window/ door frames	44	1
inside re-plastering	41	2
guttering repaired	41	2
repair garden walls	16	2
paving entries	6	2
paving front garden	11	1
build extension	8	1
internal structural change	12	–
external structural work	3	–
other repairs	21	1
no repairs done	16	–
no repairs intended	62	–
no repairs specified	–	89
no work done by council	–	–

Source: Survey.

Table 6.3
Repair and Maintenance Expenditure in Birmingham and Liverpool

| | Recent buyers | | Longer established |
	Birmingham	Liverpool	buyers (Birmingham)
Total spent (£)	443,854	266,834	229,579
per household (£)	577	1,253	1,435
of which:	%	%	%
improvement grants	14	21	19
loans	13	15	26
household savings	73	64	55
Total	100	100	100

Source: Survey.

balance, excluding improvement grants, being raised in the form of loans.

Improvement grants amounted then to only a small proportion of a relatively small sum of money. Thus, for example, the per capita value of improvement grants was only £81 among Birmingham recent buyers. However, this is partly because only a small minority of households obtained improvements grants. (We do not know whether this was because they did not apply or failed to obtain one.) It is therefore more useful to examine the per capita value of improvement grants among only those households who received them. Once again, however, it is necessary to stress that the sums involved are only rough indications. It is also necessary to bear in mind that not only is the level of improvement grant activity affected by 'take up' but the size of grants given is affected by the scale and nature of the improvements undertaken, the type of grant given, the circumstances of the occupant and whether the dwelling is the subject of area action. The overall quantity of grant money available is also subject to the allocation of resources to, and within, a local authority's Housing Investment Programme.

Table 6.4 shows the total expenditure on grants and the proportion they represented of total improvement and repair expenditure, analysed according to the size of individual grants. It can be seen that while the median amount of grant was between £1,000 and £1,999 among recent and longer-established buyers in Birmingham, among Liverpool recent buyers it was over £2,000. Furthermore, grants rose as a percentage of total expenditure as the size of grant increased from around 10 per cent for grants under £500 to over half for grants over £2,000.

The data on repairs and maintenance carried out by buyers were supplemented by a range of attitudinal data collected during the questionnaire surveys and from in-depth interviews conducted with a number of recent buyers in Birmingham whose houses were included in the condition survey. These data provided us with some insights into the ways in which households were coping with repairs and maintenance, and allowed us to place their actual patterns of behaviour and expenditure into the context of their personal lives.

Table 6.4 :   Size of Improvement Grants in Relation to Total Grant-aided Expenditure

in Inner Birmingham and Liverpool

| Size of grant (£) | Inner Birmingham | | | | | | | | Inner Liverpool | | | |
| | Recent Buyers[1] | | | | Longer-established Buyers[2] | | | | Recent Buyers[1] | | | |
	No. of grant aided households	Total Value of grants	Mean value of grant	grant as % of total spend	No of grant aided households	Total value of grants	Mean value of grant	grant as % of total spend	No of grant-aided households	Total value of grants	mean value	grant as % of total spend
	No.	£	£	%	No.	£	£	%	No.	£	£	%
under 500	13	1,987	153	12	5	700	140	12	2	89	45	9
500-999	8	5,229	654	37	6	4,400	733	26	-	-	-	-
1000-1,900	16	23,750	1,484	47	9	12,690	1,410	36	8	12,254	1,532	41
2,000 or more	13	44,762	3,443	61	8	25,300	3,163	38	12	40,100	3,350	59
Total	50[3]	75,726	1,515	49	28[4]	43,090	1,539	34	22[5]	52,443	2,384	47
Incomplete data	5	-	-	-	-	-	-	-	1	-	-	-

Sources: 1. Recent Buyers Surveys Birmingham and Liverpool
2. Re-interview survey of Birmingham buyers
3. 55 grant-aided households or 7.2% of buyers
4. 28 grant-aided households or 13.9% of longer-established buyers
5. 23 grant-aided households or 10.8 percent of buyers

A number of points emerged. First, the very large scale of the problem of coping with disrepair was all too apparent. Over half of all the longer-established buyers had postponed carrying out items of major repair work, mostly because they were unable to afford it. For many longer-established buyers, expenditure on repairs and maintenance had necessitated cutting back drastically or completely on other major items such as holidays or the use or purchase of a car. In one or two cases it was clear that severe domestic and marital strains had occurred in the household, as a result of the domestic disorder of repair work, the costs of meeting repairs or the consequences of not being able to carry out urgent repair work.

'If we had known the bad state of repair the house was in we wouldn't have bought it. Plus, now we have two children, one of each sex, but only two bedrooms. To cap it all we have since been offered a three bedroom council house with a garden, which was what we wanted originally.'

'Well, we haven't coped with repairs because my wife has had to go back to work to help with the money because of the rewiring costing so much. We have got another five years on that loan still to pay.'

'We scrape along and if desperate we miss the mortgage repayments. The bathroom ceiling has fallen down with too much steam.'

'My savings are being spent on the house. I have had to do without a holiday because of getting the repairs done.'

For half of all longer-established buyers, repairs were singled out as the most serious problem with their housing, and of these, half indicated that they thought repairs would become an increasing problem as time passed. Furthermore, longer-established buyers appeared to hold a rather pessimistic view of their ability to cope with repairs. A third of all households thought that if they ran into financial difficulties in the future they would simply have to neglect any disrepair, while a further 15 per cent said that they would try to sell the house. As one householder who couldn't cope with repairs and was selling the house put it: 'You don't know how things will turn out. It was supposed to be an investment.' Only 6 per cent said they would apply for a council tenancy. (In fact, at the time of writing, Birmingham does not accept owner-occupiers on its housing register).

The pessimism of households concerning their ability to cope with repairs cropped up again and again in interviews with buyers. The combination of expense, discomfort and household disorganisation which major repairs involve placed a continual and seemingly endless strain on households. Thus, repairs and maintenance were stated to be the major disadvantage of having bought rather than rented, of having bought an old rather than a newer house and of having bought the particular house itself. It was also stated as a major reason for wanting to move, and was an important factor among those who seriously considered taking action to sell.

'I regret having bought an old house. It needs too much spent on repairs. You have to spend a lot of money and still its never worth it if you try to sell.'

'Two years ago we asked the council to buy our house, and filled in a form for selling it to the council. We have just recently heard that they've refused to buy it.'

'I think everyone would like a nice new house, but it depends on circumstances - old houses are cheaper to buy.'

The overall picture in both cities is that buyers make a considerable personal sacrifice in order to attempt to keep up with the problem of disrepair. It is interesting to compare the reactions of Birmingham buyers with Anfield buyers (Tables 6.5 and 6.6). The fact that in Anfield the standard of housing was clearly worse than in the Birmingham areas and that Anfield buyers had spent more on repairs and maintenance than had Birmingham buyers might suggest that the problem of disrepair may well be even worse in Liverpool than in Birmingham, at least in terms of its effect on the households. In fact fewer Liverpool buyers were worried by repairs, probably because Anfield buyers were slightly better off than Birmingham buyers, had smaller families, cheaper houses and longer term loans with smaller monthly repayments. This suggests that income and financial obligations were the crucial factors in determining whether or not repairs were a burden. Even so similar kinds of problems faced many Liverpool buyers:

'My wife has had to take a part time job to cope with the cost of repairs.'

'We are finding it difficult to cope with repairs. Well, the house consumes all my money. I am struggling along trying to get the repairs done.'

'Its falling apart. The main drains in the street have subsided and caused cracks to this property. This only happened in the past two weeks.'

'I only bought such an old house because I just couldn't get anywhere with the corporation. I wanted a ground floor flat because of my mother's ill health.'

The survey questions analysed so far in this chapter provide us with information on repair activities and on attitudes to repair work but tell us little about the actual condition of the housing. The condition survey was therefore designed to obtain quantitative measures of the state of disrepair of recent buyers' houses in inner Birmingham. The schedule was based on that used in the English House Condition Surveys of 1976 and 1981.

As indicated earlier, the condition survey was based on a one in five sample of the houses included in the recent buyers surveys of the four Birmingham areas. This sample, duly weighted, provided a cross-section of the stock of houses bought between 1975 and 1979, ranging from the worst houses in Saltley to the newest post-1919 houses in Handsworth.

Table 6.5

Repair Problems of Recent Buyers in Inner Birmingham and Liverpool

Repair problems	Birmingham	Anfield, Liverpool
	%	%
no problem	64	72
do it self, as and when needed	5	1
do it in turn as affordable	11	9
saving and will apply for grant	2	1
don't know how will manage	4	11
will borrow informally (mainly Pakistanis)	2	2
waiting for grant	3	1
will wait till loans repaid	5	1
other	4	2
don't know, no reply	1	–
Total	100	100

Source: Survey.

Table 6.6

Repairs Postponed by Recent Buyers in Inner Birmingham and Liverpool

Proportions of buyers mentioning postponing repairs to:	Birmingham	Anfield, Liverpool
	%	%
roof/guttering	12	16
chimneys	2	3
bath/bathroom	8	4
damp proofing	6	8
inside toilet	3	–
rewiring	3	4
windows	10	8
cosmetics	5	–
replaster walls	14	5
none or other	52	67

* Percentages add up to more than 100 because up to three items could be mentioned.

Source: Survey.

Table 6.7 Condition of the Fabric of Dwellings Purchased by Recent Buyers in Inner Birmingham (1981 Condition Survey)

					No reply	Total
Foundations	Good condition no evidence of settlement	Some settlement; no longer active	some settlement; needs work; broken lintels, sills or bricks; insufficient foundations	major settlement; broken arches, cracks in main structure, wings separated from main structure		
%	9	63	25	1	2	100
External walls	good condition	minor defects in painting localised cracking or cracking bricks	perished + broken brickwork, missing bricks, localised bulging defective arches, expensive areas of defective rendering			
%	15	67	16		2	100
External doors + windows	good condition painted in last 3 years to good standard woodwork in good condition	paint covers all timberwork, no blistering or exposed areas some Rotted wood.	Timber exposed in some parts. Broken or loose window panes defective woodwork	timber exposed in many parts. Defective or rotten woodwork in some doors + windows		
%	16	63	18	1	2	100
Chimney stacks	good condition	defective pointing flashing, flashing cross pots	perished, broken brickwork with defective poining, flashing flaunching slight lean			
%	14	70	13		3	100
Roof covering	good condition	few slates missing/cracked defective flashing	patches of slates broken or missing			
%	14	67	17		2	100
Roof structure	good condition	slight deformation of ridge + pitch	extensive deformation of ridge + pitch			
%	15	76	7		2	100
Roof drainage	good condition	insecure but sound rain-water goods, missing end plate. Insufficient fall. Blockage or not discharging over gully	Some rusted broken leaking gutters or downpipes	extensively rusted broken, leaking gutters + downpipes		
%	15	57	23	3	2	100
Dampness	damp proof course working effectively	some evidence of failure or bridgeing of DP course	general or extensive dampness to walls	no-damp proof course		
%	2	14	76	8	2	100
Extension structure	good condition sound construction materials conform with building regulations	well-maintained but poor disposition substandard materials	poor condition or repair poor disposition sub-standard materials	ramshackle conversion of original outbuildings	-	
%(No extension 64%)	19	9	3	2	3	100

Source: Survey

Table 6.7 shows the physical condition of these houses. It can be seen that only a small minority of houses was in good condition in any one respect. External doors and windows were the parts of the fabric in best condition with 16 per cent of dwellings classified as in good condition. Dampness was the worst problem; only 2 per cent of dwellings had a damp proof course which was working effectively and 8 per cent had no damp proof course at all. Between a half and three-quarters of dwellings could be described as possessing a number of minor or major defects. These included pointing defects, rotten woodwork, loose chimney pots and defective stacks, missing or loose roof slates, deformed roof structure, insecure or blocked roof drainage, and extensive dampness to the walls.

A further 10 to 25 per cent of dwellings possessed major structural defects, including bulging external walls, exposed and defective woodwork in doors and windows, leaning chimney stacks, patches of missing or broken roof slates, extensive deformation of roof structures, rusted, broken and leaking guttering, and no damp proof course. Rear extensions also exhibited a high incidence of defects. Of the 36 per cent of dwellings with an extension, only half were in good condition and conformed with building regulations. The remainder were either built with substandard materials, were poorly maintained or were ramshackle conversions of external out-buildings.

The high incidence of disrepair was also estimated in terms of the amount of repair or renewal work which was required to bring the fabric up to a 30 year life standard. Table 6.8 summarises these findings. It can be seen that the proportion of dwellings which required no

Table 6.8
Repairs Required for 30 Year Life: Birmingham (1981 Condition Survey)

Repairs Required to:		None (0%)	Some (15%)	Much (40%)	Most (75%)	Completely (100%)	No data or not applicable	Total
					Amount of renewal needed			
foundations	(%)	14	60	23	2	0	1	100
external walls	(%)	16	61	21	0	0	2	100
external door + windows	(%)	14	56	28	3	0	0	100
chimney stacks	(%)	12	59	25	2	0	2	100
roof covering	(%)	13	12	33	33	9	0	100
roof structure	(%)	15	29	44	10	2	0	100
roof drainage	(%)	14	33	19	18	15	1	100
dampness	(%)	11	24	41	18	4	2	100
extension structure	(%)	6	14	4	4	–	72	100

Source: Survey.

renewal work at all in any one aspect ranged upwards from 11 per cent
requiring no work to rectify dampness to 16 per cent requiring no work
on external walls. Most houses required either some work (15 per cent
renewal) or much work (40 per cent renewal) on at least one and often
several parts of their fabric. Roof covering was the most defective of
all, with 75 per cent of dwellings requiring 40 per cent or more
renewal work, and 42 per cent of dwellings requiring 75 per cent or
more roof renewal. Roof structure and roof drainage also required
considerable work. The other major renewal work needed was damp
proofing, with 22 per cent of dwellings requiring at least 75 per cent
renewal work.

The cost of carrying out these improvements to bring the whole
dwelling up to a 30 year life standard including amenities was also
estimated (see Table 6.9). It can be seen that costs tended to group
around £3,000 or £10,000; the mean cost of improving the stock of
dwellings to a 30 year life standard was at £6,872. Only 7 per cent of
properties required less than £500 spent in improvements, and 16 per
cent less than £1,500 while 10 per cent required no less than £12,500
to be spent. The cost of correcting the disrepair of this stock of
dwellings is therefore very considerable.

Table 6.9
Estimated Cost of Improvement to 30 Year Standard : Birmingham
(1981 Condition Survey)

Cost	Dwellings	Mean	£	Weighted total
£	%			
under 500	7	For whole stock	6,872	153
500 - 1,499	9	For all costing		
1,500 - 2,499	8	over £500	7,424	137
2,500 - 3,499	14	For all pre-1919	7,562	130
3,500 - 4,499	7	For all pre-1919		
4,500 - 5,499	1	costing over £500	7,741	127
5,500 - 6,499	-	For all post-1919	2,222	17
6,500 - 7,499	3	For all post-1919		
7,500 - 8,499	5	costing over £500	3,636	11
8,500 - 9,499	6			
9,500 - 10,499	13			
10,500 - 11,499	7			
11,500 - 12,499	8			
12,500 - 13,499	4			
13,500 - 14,499	6			
no data	3			
Total	100			
Weighted N =	153			

Table 6.10
Mean House Price and Estimated Cost of Improvement needed for 30 year
life: Birmingham (1981 Condition Survey)

% of cases	Estimated cost of improvement (£)	Mean house price (£)	Mean house price plus estimated improvement cost (£)
%	£	£	£
6	0	7,428	7,428
38	under 5,000	6,190	8,581
16	between 5,000 and 10,000	5,497	13,186
40	over 10,000	4,155	15,698
100	6,872	5,363	12,235

These costs must be compared with the price paid for the dwellings (Table 6.10). The mean price paid between 1975 and 1979 was £5,363 or 22 per cent less than the estimated mean cost of improvement to a 30 year life in 1981. The total mean purchase price plus mean improvement cost was £12,235, though, on the 40 per cent of the stock which required over £10,000 spent on improvements, the total mean purchase price plus improvement cost was £15,698. This excludes improvement expenditure already incurred between the purchase of the property and the date at which our condition survey was done.

A comparison between the pre-1919 housing and the inter and post-war housing is also interesting (see Table 6.9). It can be seen that although the amount of repair expenditure needed was much lower than for pre-1919 housing, these houses are far from being in a perfect condition. Thus, the mean cost of improving all 17 of the post-1919 houses surveyed was £2,222, and of those only six required work costing under £500. The mean cost of improving the 11 houses needing over £500 spent was £3,636. This was 47 per cent of the amount needed to improve all pre-1919 houses requiring over £500 work carried out. It is therefore clear that although the inter-war stock in our sample was in considerably better condition that the pre-1919 stock it was, nevertheless, in an appreciably bad state of disrepair. This is in line with other recent findings, that the inter-war stock, and especially that built in the early inter-war years, is becoming urgently in need of investment. For example, the Greater London House Condition survey found that 21 per cent of all unfit owner-occupied dwellings were in the inter-war stock (Greater London Council, 1981: 102) and preliminary results from the 1981 West Midlands House Condition survey indicate that there are two thousand unfit inter-war owner-occupied houses in Birmingham (West Midlands County Council, 1982).

The general condition of the housing stock can be summed up in terms of legislative criteria of unfitness: that is, the extent to which the housing stock falls short of certain minimum standards of fitness as set out in legislation. Tables 6.11a and 6.11b present estimates in terms of the Housing Act 1957 and the Public Health Acts. It can be seen that 5 per cent of pre-1919 dwellings were, under the 1957 Housing Act, deemed to be unfit, 79 per cent were fit but required some action and only 12 per cent were fit and required no action. Similarly, under the Public Health Acts, while 5 per cent of the pre-1919 stock would be liable for action, a further 26 per cent would probably be liable and only 11 per cent would definitely not be liable. In the inter-war stock levels of unfitness were naturally very much lower, but still 10 to 20 per cent of the stock was considered to require action under one or other piece of legislation.

Given the very large sums which are required to bring these houses up to a 30 year life standard and given the very meagre financial resources available to their owners, it is almost inevitable that at current levels of improvement activity the housing stock will deteriorate further. Ultimately, the cost of improving to a 30 year life may become so great, that it becomes economically wiser to demolish rather than improve. This is the situation already arrived at in parts of Saltley, in the view of the city's urban renewal officers.

A very serious issue, which arises from the very high cost of improvement in relation to purchase price, is the 'valuation gap'. This is the difference between what a house costs to purchase and improve and the price that the improved house will fetch on the open market. Many houses in the inner city which have been improved will not sell for a price which covers the cost of purchase and improvement at current prices even allowing for current levels of grant. This means that if owners have to sell quickly after they have improved, they will risk making a loss. The risk of this happening may well deter people from improving. The City of Birmingham in its Purchase and Improvement Mortgage Scheme (PIMS)[3] has found that when houses are recently acquired the valuation gap 'may be £6000 – £10,000' (Edwards, 1982: 14). Average improvement costs under PIMS in the period 1978/9 were £10,500 yet all the houses covered by the scheme in that period were valued and sold at less than £10,000 improved. Part of the loss on PIMS (up to £3,875 per house) was met by central government and the remainder, on average £2,000 per house, was met by the city. The apparent loss has been kept down because the city has owned many of the properties for many years and on average paid only £1,500 for each. The real loss to the city, which would have to take account of the price at which the houses would now sell unimproved (the opportunity cost), is of course much greater.

The problem of the valuation gap is a very difficult one. The high price of unimproved property reflects high demand from low income owners for relatively cheap inner city property whether improved or unimproved, while the low price of inner city improved property reflects both the lack of demand for them (outside London) by higher income classes and the fact that inner city houses are handicapped by an 'area price', reflecting environmental features, lending institution attitudes and in some areas, race attitudes as well. Higher grants,

Table 6.11a : Fitness According to the Housing Act 1957: Birmingham

Age of houses	Fit, no action	Fit S.9 1A and 1B	Fit S.9 part III added	Unfit part III single	Unfit part III area	Not Known Can't Estimate	Total
Pre-1919 houses %	12	78	1	3	2	4	100 (N=135)
Post-1919 houses %	72	17	17	-	-		100 (N=18)
Total %	19	71	1	3	2	4	100 (N=153)

Table 6.11b : Fitness According to Public Health Acts: Birmingham

Age of houses	Action liable					Total
	No action	Probably none	Probably action	Action	Not Known Can't Estimate	
Pre-1919 %	11	52	26	5	6	100 (N=135)
Post-1919 %	78	11	-	1	10	100 (N=18)
Total %	19	48	23	5	5	100 (N=153)

Source: Survey

PIM schemes or enveloping (see below) are all ways of trying to tackle the valuation gap problem while attempting to retain the property in owner-occupation.

To return to our survey of condition and improvements, one very important finding was that households were seriously under-estimating the amount of work which their houses required in order to bring them up to a minimum standard. Table 6.12 shows the amount of renewal work needed on selected items, according to the condition survey, for all dwellings where the householders claimed that no renewal was needed of those same items. It can be seen that despite their owner's opinion only a small minority of the houses were considered by the public health officer doing the condition survey to be in a good condition and not requiring work done. There is clearly a great discrepancy between the buyers' estimates of work needed and those of the survey. These were not exceptional cases; 95 per cent of all owners of property in the condition survey said nothing needed doing to their chimneys; and 88 per cent said nothing needed doing to the roof or to remedy damp. Two cases studies indicate the extent of the discrepancy:

A couple with six children had bought a three bedroom house in 1978 for £4,500 using £3,150 from the sale of their previous house plus savings. According to the condition survey the property was in poor condition in 1981. The roof covering and drainage needed completely renewing, the roof structure needed 75 per cent renewing and minor repairs were needed on all other parts of the fabric. In total the cost of these repairs was estimated at £11,000. When asked what repairs or improvements needed doing, the owner felt that of the list of items he was asked to choose from, the only work needed was on replacing doors and window frames.

A couple with five children and two lodgers had bought a five bedroomed house on a 23 year lease for £6,000 in 1979 using a £3,000 bank loan and £3,000 from the sale of their previous house. They had spent £1,800 on rewiring, re-flooring, treating woodwork, replacing window frames, re-plastering, re-guttering and installing a new bath, but indicated that the other items - damp proof course, pointing, tiling and chimneys did not require any attention. The condition survey found that in 1981 a total of no less than £14,000 was required to be spent to bring the property up to a 30 year life including renewing 75 per cent of the damp proof course and 40 per cent of the external walls, roof covering and roof structure, as well as minor repairs to all other parts of the fabric.

In summary, then, the findings on house condition in Anfield and inner Birmingham are profoundly disquieting. The owner-occupiers of the stock possess limited financial resources and experience great difficulty in carrying out repairs. Nonetheless they expend what are for them large amounts of money, raised at great personal sacrifice. In spite of this the amount of repair work being carried out by both recent and longer-established buyers was of a relatively modest cosmetic type in comparison with the repairs needed. Only a small minority of households had carried out repairs using improvement grants totalling between a third and a half of total expenditure. The Birmingham condition survey showed that the stock is in a very serious state of disrepair, with large amounts of renewal work required on most

Table 6.12
Work required on specific items to ensure a 30 year life:
all dwellings where household estimated that no work was required:
Birmingham

Condition survey estimate of renewal work required for a 30 year life in 1981 [1]	Roof covering	Chimney Stacks	Guttering	Dampess
	%	%	%	%
Good nil	14	14	15	11
15% renewal required	11	56	36	26
40%	30	26	20	41
75%	36	2	16	19
100%	8	–	14	2
No information	–	2	–	2
Total	100	100	100	100
Number of dwellings about which owners said no work was need on this item [2] N =	131	146	135	132
Those dwellings as percentage of total	86	95	88	86

1. Source: 1981 condition survey (sub-sample of 1979 recent buyers survey)

2. Source: 1979 recent buyers survey – work either not needed or defect subsequently remedied by householder.

houses at a cost which would be far in excess of the owner-occupier's resources and on average even more than the buyers paid for the house. The net result of this is that while the great majority of houses are still fit, they nevertheless fall below minimum legislative standards, and if they are not soon improved substantially, much of the stock may well become unfit in the near future.

Though our condition survey covered only the four areas of inner Birmingham, our findings cannot be regarded as unrepresentative of the problems of Birmingham's inner city or of Liverpool's, or indeed of inner areas in other major British cities. In particular our findings are unlikely to exaggerate the problems because the areas we chose for study were, if anything, biased towards the newer end of the pre-1919 stock. [4] With the progress made by housing associations and local authorities in the rehabilitation of their own pre-1919 inner city rental stock, it is the owner-occupied sector in inner city areas in which there is now the most visible deterioration in state of repair. For instance a preliminary report by the West Midlands County Council on the West Midlands 1981 House Condition Survey stated: 'The problem of unfit housing is concentrated in the owner-occupied sector. For example; in Birmingham 46 per cent of unfits are owner-occupied and 17 per cent privately rented' (West Midlands County Council, 1982 4.5). Similarly Friend has written of Liverpool,

'The overall housing standard has clearly improved, but with one in five properties still to be dealt with, it is the owner-occupied houses in the main which are the sore thumbs. The vast bulk of the former privately rented properties are now in housing association ownership, while a smaller number have either been improved by landlords themselves or acquired by the local authority' (Friend, 1981 p 39).

It is clear from research on area improvement that the administrative and financial measures so far implemented to try to achieve improvement of the older housing stock have been far more successful in the publicly owned rental sector than in the low income owner-occupied sector. This is not surprising since the subsidies per house improved in these sectors have been much greater than in the private sector. This is ironical given the low incomes upon which inner city owner-occupiers have to base their renewal efforts. The implication of this is that much greater public investment in private sector renewal will be required if cities like Birmingham and Liverpool are to be able to improve their inner city housing without taking much larger amounts of it into public ownership. In the next chapter we will go on to consider this issue and other policy implications of this report.

NOTES

(1) The term 'recent buyers' throughout this report refers to people who were included in the 'recent buyers surveys', i.e. buyers between 1975 and 1979.

(2) The terms 'longer-established' or 'longer-term buyers' refer to people included in the re-interview surveys of Saltley, Soho and Sparkhill. They were people who bought between 1972 and 1974 and were still in the same house in 1980.

(3) This scheme involves the city in purchasing and improving property for sale. The sale price is the improved value and is normally less than the cost of purchase and improvement.

(4) The house condition survey carried out in Birmingham as a supplement to the 1981 English House Condition Survey found even more serious levels of unfitness in the pre-1919 owner-occupied stock than we found in one sample. This must be partly a result of our taking the upper end of the stock and partly a matter of varying interpretation of the same conditions.

7 The privatisation of squalor

This study has documented the variety and scale of the problems associated with lower income home ownership in five inner city areas, four in Birmingham and one in Liverpool. The problems include falling relative property values, the lack of conventional mortgage lending at the bottom of the inner city housing market, the vulnerability of buyers, particularly ethnic minority buyers to prejudicial practices by market professionals, and a state of disrepair which is beyond the resources of buyers to remedy. Moreover, the evidence indicates that the market is working to produce greater rather than less differentiation between this bottom segment of property and the bulk of the market, in terms of house prices, property conditions, sources of finance, the incomes of buyers and, in Birmingham, their ethnic origins. The implications of these trends are considerable because they indicate the emergence of ghetto like conditions within the home-ownership sector with far-reaching effects on race relations and social mobility. In terms of housing policy our findings raise a whole series of questions regarding reliance upon an urban renewal strategy based on publicly subsidised private initiatives.

In this concluding chapter we consider the implications of the evidence gathered in this study. Our assessment is pessimistic, not because we wish to condemn home ownership as a tenure, but rather because the proponents of that tenure seem incapable of acknowledging the problems that exist and are therefore unwilling to develop appropriate policies. To counterbalance this tendency we devote considerable attention to the policy issues and options which arise. We begin with a brief discussion of the market differentiation we have observed. We then proceed to a consideration of policy issues in the light of the main findings of our study. Finally we consider the prospects for low income home-ownership, the inner city and for the social and economic structure of British society.

The emergence of wide differentials within the housing market, between the best housing and the worst, are clearly in line with what we might expect to happen in a totally unregulated market. The ever-expanding horizons of luxury accommodation sit remarkably comfortably alongside the steadily worsening situation of some inner city housing and its occupants. Filtering theory, the long term proposition of free-market economists, would suggest that the expanding supply of good quality homes will result in the release of accommodation of moderate quality and price which itself will filter down 'to low income purchasers. The low income purchasers will filter up' on the backs of the capital gains they have made on their existing property and their enhanced earning power. Such a comforting scenario sits uneasily with the realities we have identified in this study. In Birmingham there is little evidence that new construction of middle and upper income homes generates any surplus stock which filters downwards. The housing market is simply much more complex and stratified than that theory would predict (see Boddy and Gray, 1979 for a useful discussion of filtering). Equally, the widening differential in prices and the high incidence of unemployment or reduced earnings amongst inner city dwellers has meant that the opportunities for upward filtering are diminishing day by day. The position in Liverpool is less acute. There, the bottom end of the market appears to function in a way more commensurate with filtering theory's ladder, but that may be because of the smaller supply of owner-occupied housing available in Liverpool's inner city.

If the Birmingham situation is repeated elsewhere, and there are good reasons for believing it is not and certainly will not in the future be confined to that city alone, then home ownership far from being a springboard becomes a trap. Furthermore, given the conditions we have described, it is a squalid trap. Unlike many owners who might expect capital gains on their property and the possibility of movement to a different strata of the market, these owners may suffer real capital losses and far from being able to move they will be forced to stay in a deteriorating asset which will be in a deteriorating condition. In addition, with the rapid escalation of council house sales a whole new stratum of low income housing is being placed on the market undercutting the inner areas and diverting potential purchasers elsewhere. Faced with a choice of a suburban ex-council house or an inner city slum, it is plain which many buyers will choose. The routes out therefore are diminishing, raising the possibility that ultimately these areas can only adequately be improved by massive clearance. Unlike previous eras, however, that clearance will be fragmented as the numerous individual owners bargain for their compensation (in the past block holdings from landlords simplified the process). One wonders, too, whether the massive assault on home owners (albeit low income home owners) this implies will be acceptable to those concerned with the image of that tenure. We develop these thoughts later in the chapter.

The complexities of the situation are such that a whole series of policy issues arise. However it is quite clear that the kinds of policy recommendations which can be made depend on what view is taken of the housing market. If declining inner city housing is seen as an unfortunate but inescapable or even necessary consequence of the working of the market, then clearly the kinds of policy issues which are of interest will be restricted. If, on the other hand, it is deemed that the role of government is to counteract undesirable tendencies produced by market forces then a more interventionist policy may be more appropriate. Recognising the political and economic realities of the present time we direct our attention to medium term proposals which accept that a) there will be a continuation of low-income home-ownership as the major tenure form in these areas and b) that the larger part of the housing stock in those areas will remain standing for another 30 years. Even within this narrowly defined brief, we still have to discuss, first, the broad policy issues surrounding mortgage lending arrangements and the role of market institutions and, second, the implications of low income home ownership for urban renewal. These two issues are inter-related. Policies to improve the inner city housing stock cannot be separated from policies related to mortgage lending nor from the intersection between low incomes and poor housing. However, it is convenient to divide up discussion in this way, bearing in mind that the policy areas are interdependent and that the neglect of one can undermine active remedial measures in another. In addressing these issues we need first to reconsider the main findings of the study.

SUMMARY OF MAIN FINDINGS

In Birmingham we found that there were marked differences between buyers of different ethnic origins. Indian and especially Pakistani buyers tended to have larger families, to have owned a house previously, and to buy low-priced, leasehold houses with unconventional finance. British, Irish and West Indian buyers tended to have small families, to be first-time buyers and to have bought higher-priced freehold houses with conventional finance.

Between 1975 and 1979 house prices in the four inner Birmingham areas and in Anfield, Liverpool, while increasing in money terms, fell by about 15 per cent relative to the respective regional means. In Saltley, Soho and Sparkhill, for which prices were available from 1972, prices fell by about 25 per cent relative to the West Midlands mean, between 1972 and 1979. Inner area prices also lagged behind the mean for pre-1919 terraced houses in the region which had been mortgaged by building societies over the same period.

Differences between the mean house prices of the different inner Birmingham areas increased between 1972 and 1979. Price differences between the newer and older houses within areas in both Birmingham and Liverpool also increased. Thus, for instance, house prices in housing action areas in Anfield rose more slowly than the Anfield mean. Similarly pre-1919 house prices rose more slowly than post-1919 house prices in Handsworth.

Conventional lending increased marginally in inner Birmingham between 1972 and 1979, but building society lending remained largely confined to the highest priced houses, and disproportionately among British, Irish and West Indian buyers. Informal lending increased among Asian buyers of the lowest priced houses. Finance company lending declined sharply but short-term lending by the clearing banks remained very high.

Informal market organisation is a particular feature of inner city buying especially when Asians are involved in buying houses for cash or with non-conventional mortgages. Amongst ethnic minorities there is a heavy dependence on community contacts.

There were marked differences between building societies and between branches of the same society as to the number of loan applications received and the number granted in any one inner city area. Some building societies received much larger numbers of mortgage requests than others did. Some granted a very large proportion of applicants' requests while others granted very few. Some building societies lent fairly freely in one area but very little in another. The role of solicitors and estate agents in channelling mortgages to applicants appears to be crucial.

The impact of these lending decisions appears to affect ethnic minorities adversely. They also tend to receive less help from market professionals. The causes of this disadvantageous treatment range through the quality of the property, the incomes of borrowers, their knowledge of the system and finally prejudices, both of borrowers and lenders, about certain areas and certain minority groups.

The house condition survey of the inner Birmingham houses revealed a severe state of disrepair; the great majority of properties would technically qualify under the legislation for compulsory action to bring them up to minimum standards. Buyers had very little conception of the severe state of disrepair of their property.

The estimated mean cost of improvement to a 30 year life was more than the mean price paid for the houses by buyers between 1975 and 1979. Though households spent what were for them considerable amounts of money on repairs, often at great personal sacrifice, the amounts spent were far below those required to bring the houses up to a 30 year life. In addition, levels of grant-aided work were low, even among longer-established buyers.

THE IMPACT OF SHORT TERM LENDING: POLICY IMPLICATIONS

These findings raise a series of policy questions. The first concerns the nature of lending for house purchase and the prevalence of short-term loans. In this study we have found that there is very great diversity in the extent to which inner city areas and the groups buying there obtain conventional building society or local authority mortgages. In particular we have shown how dependent parts of the Birmingham housing market currently are upon the ability and willingness of Asians to buy with short-term loans from banks or friends and relations. We have to ask ourselves, first, 'does this matter?' and second, 'if it matters, what can be done about it?'

On the positive side, it is true that a proportion of buyers said they actively preferred short-term loans. By this means they could pay off their debt quickly and become the outright owners of their property. By having heavy outgoings for a short time, they would minimise them thereafter. Should they want or have to move, they would have the maximum cash-in-hand from the sale. In case of unemployment, for instance, they would not have mortgage debt to worry about. At the very worst, should the property be compulsorily purchased for demolition, they would not have an outstanding mortgage to be paid off.

In addition, though short-term bank loans have higher interest rates, the total sum of the interest paid on a 25 year loan is very much higher than the total paid on a five or seven year loan. Against this it may be argued that interest rates on long-term loans, allowing for tax relief, have often been lower than the rate of inflation, and so buyers who have taken out conventional term mortgages may actually have been financially better off than buyers who purchased outright or with very short-term loans. This argument applies less these days when inflation is low and real interest rates correspondingly higher.

Other positive advantages of short-term personal loans for the buyers are that loans are quick, the legal fees and other transaction costs are much lower, buyers are not asked to make further expenditure to remedy defects in the house, and problems such as short leases are not an obstacle to lending. In the case of loans from friends and relations, there are the added advantages that these lenders may be willing to make very flexible repayment arrangements taking into account the personal situation of the borrower. In most cases friends or relations do not charge interest, though there is often an obligation on borrowers to lend in the same way when they can. This means that the cheapness of their own loan will ultimately be offset by interest foregone on their own lending. It still means borrowing is cheap, though against this has to be weighed the fact that no subsidy through tax relief is obtained.

Short-term loans therefore have a number of attractions for buyers, particularly those least familiar with the intricacies of rates of inflation, interest rates and tax relief. What then are the negative aspects of such lending? First must come the size of the monthly repayments. Buyers of cheap inner city properties, with short-term loans find themselves paying monthly payments as high as those of buyers of property two or three times as expensive. A building society or local authority would certainly consider their incomes inadequate to meet such repayments. The ways in which they manage to pay these loans are by saving up a large deposit and so minimising the initial loan, by taking on additional evening jobs, postponing other expenditure on the house, foregoing holidays, cars and consumer durables, and sometimes by taking in lodgers. This is all right until unemployment, sickness or increased financial obligations intervene. The high level of repayments therefore produces a continuous strain on the household budget, albeit for only about five years, and it also leaves no margin for coping with financial emergencies. A second loan to meet a crisis merely increases the monthly outgoings.

Because short-term loans mean high monthly payments on relatively low-priced houses, those who use this type of financing generally confine their purchasing to the cheapest houses available, namely the oldest and in worst repair.

The lack of flexibility in budgets created by high monthly repayments has particular implications when properties are in poor state of repair. Households will, during the loan period, have very little money for repairs and maintenance. This is shown up most clearly when there is a major failure such as a roof, chimney or ceiling collapse but it applies in a less dramatic way to routine repairs and maintenance. Though it can be argued that buyers soon become outright owners and are then well able to do improvements, this situation does not necessarily last long because buyers move on and sell the property. The new buyer with a short-term loan will be in the same position as the old buyer, deferring repairs until the loan is paid off. And so it goes on. For the local authority, concerned about the condition of the inner city stock and anxious to encourage owners to take out grants and loans for improvement, the prevalence of short-term lending must be a source of considerable worry.

A third problem brought about by dependence on short-term loans is that many people will not buy at all if this is the only form of lending available. Perfectly legitimately, they do not want to take the risk or make the extreme sacrifices in other aspects of their living standards that monthly payments at this level require. So faced with a refusal from conventional mortgage lenders they will either buy in an area where mortgages are more readily available or they will rent instead. The results of this are that some people have to buy in areas they do not like; that better-off buyers who can obtain conventional mortgages on newer, more expensive houses in the suburbs will be 'steered' towards these, even if they would have preferred to buy and improve inner city property; that there will be a concentration in inner city areas of those people who are willing to borrow short-term loans but whose income would not, on the criteria adopted by the building societies, allow them to get a mortgage on a suburban property. West Indians and whites are less likely than Asians to accept short-term loans, and tend to move into council housing when they fail to obtain a conventional mortgage on a cheap house. It appears that this is a factor in increasing the marked concentration of Asian buyers in cheaper inner city property. By 1981, the concentrations of black households in the four Birmingham survey areas were much more marked than they had been in 1971. The proportions of households with the head born in the New Commonwealth and Pakistan were as follows, in 1971 and 1981 respectively: Saltley, 16.8 per cent and 34.6 per cent; Soho, 48.0 per cent and 71.1 per cent; Sparkhill, 24.5 per cent and 52.5 per cent; Handsworth, 32.6 per cent and 53.7 per cent. Soho had the heaviest concentration of any ward in Birmingham (1981 Census, County Monitors).

The end result of the dependence on short-term loans is that house prices in these areas are low, reflecting both the shortage of effective demand created by lending problems and the high monthly costs of relatively low-priced property. Though low prices are an advantage to low income buyers they deter lenders and so most of the advantage is lost, especially if high interest short-term loans are required to buy at all.

In some areas short-term loans are so prevalent that problems arise for conventional lenders in competing with them. We said earlier that short-term loans had the advantage to borrowers of being quick. As a result many estate agents will give preference to a purchaser who has a loan from a bank or relative because it will be quick and the agent's commission will be realised rapidly. This means that in some areas a buyers will be 'hustled', by the apparent competition from short-term-loan borrowers, into becoming short-term borrowers themselves. Another factor is that banks, unlike building societies, pay fees to agents who introduce borrowers to them. This inevitably has given short-term lending an added attraction for agents. However, the picture is not quite as clear as that since some agents who bring clients to the building societies charge the client for the service. This is not an officially encouraged practice but is generally accepted by societies as a fact of life which is best not enquired into.

Another reason why short-term loans are able to undermine conventional mortgages is that, as mentioned earlier, banks and friends and relations do not make repairs a condition of lending. Many people in inner cities who are offered local authority or building society loans withdraw their application when they see the cost of the required repairs. These repairs requirements, though important to the upkeep of the stock, are often enough to deter a low income buyer. The result of this is that many turn to bank or informal loans, and so the property remains unrepaired. Here we see a dilemma for conventional lenders in inner cities. Easy lending with no conditions, can mean more deteriorated stock. Careful lending with repairs conditions means less buyers altogether or more buyers with short-term loans. Both phenomena have implications for the upkeep of the stock, the maintenance of its value and the financial situation of buyers.

It seems then that there are considerable problems associated with short-term lending. Some of these, notably the level of monthly repayments, are severe problems for buyers, but certain groups, particularly Asians, are willing to trade off these disadvantages against the advantages they see of easy and quick access to a loan, lower transaction costs and the lower total cost of a house over the life of the loan. Most buyers, however, cannot or will not meet such monthly repayments with the result that they cannot buy at all if these are the only loans available. The disadvantages of short-term loans are vitally important also to the local authority, in its concern for the inner city housing stock and its loss of quality and value.

CURRENT LENDING PRACTICE AND ITS REFORM

Our survey has given us some indications of the sorts of feasible and effective changes in mortgage lending which could be introduced in inner cities. Let us first itemise the problems we have identified and then go on to see which sort of institutional arrangements might help to overcome these problems.

First, potential buyers have difficulty in identifying those building societies most likely to lend in their area, unless, by chance, they happen to choose the right one to save with, or have received help from a solicitor or estate agent. This problem is all the greater in that while some areas have reasonably good levels of conventional mortgage lending, others have scarcely any.

Second, because there are so many building societies, it is not possible to attribute to any one of them responsibility for mortgage famine in inner cities. Even the Support Lending Scheme does not guarantee that funds go to the areas most neglected by building societies.

Third, a local authority has no way of monitoring the scale of the problems being met by potential purchasers or areas in the inner city, and no way of knowing where its own funds are most needed to counteract neglect by building societies and banks. Nor do the building societies themselves know what impact local branch activities are having on paticular areas. They have no reliable means of knowing whether particular groups or areas are being refused disproportionately by their own society or by any other. This lack of management control may, or may not, be a handicap to them commercially but it certainly damages their image of being socially responsible.

Fourth, the Pakistani community, in particular, has become so entrenched in short-term bank lending that this has become the normal method of purchasing housing, whether or not it is the best method. Middle-men tend to refer aspiring purchasers to banks.

What policy initiatives could be devised to reduce, if not solve, these problems? First, we would argue that if inner city buyers are to be given greater access to conventional loans and if inner city properties are to receive higher and more consistent levels of private and public investment, it is essential that there is a much more informed and co-ordinated approach to lending in the inner city. None of the institutions involved is really adequately informed about its own lending, let alone that of other institutions. None know enough about the people whose mortgage applications fail. So our first recommendation is that the building societies, banks and local authorities inform themselves of the geographical, social and racial pattern of their own lending and refused applications. Second, building societies and banks should also determine what differences exist in lending between different branches and the extent to which these reflect the different attitudes and approaches of branch managers. Third, building societies and banks should try to establish what impact lending via solicitors and agents has on their allocations; whether stated policies of the institution, such as membership requirements, are substantially subverted in this way; and whether this means that certain types of borrower are less often helped.

The collection of information and monitoring needs to be done in such a way that the local authority can use it to establish which parts of the city and which groups are being neglected by the major lenders. Ideally some agreement needs to be reached between societies at local authorities about a standard format. Once it has this information, the local authority would be in a better position to analyse the patterns of lending and, from that, work towards a co-ordinated strategy. The major gap in its knowledge would be the informal lending sector, which, as we have seen, is a major one in Birmingham. It should, however, be possible to compare estimates of overall turnover of owner-occupied property with the data on conventional lending. The appearance of large disparities would allow the authority to see which areas were being neglected by institutional lenders. In addition material on refused applications should help to illuminate some of the reasons for this neglect, as well as the levels of applications to different types of institution in different areas and from different groups.

One of the advantages of the Support Lending Scheme has been that it has given local authorities the opportunity and justification for monitoring building society activity at least over a limited field of their activity. Thus local authorities that have been most active in monitoring information have been able to increase the success rate overall and to even out the responses of different societies (City of Plymouth 1981). Where the scheme has worked best, the local authority has also been in a position to point prospective inner city borrowers towards a more sympathetic lender. Had the local authorities the same type of information for all inner city applications and lending, and the same knowledge of building societies' and banks' willingness to lend in particular parts of an inner city, they would be in a much

better position to help prospective buyers and to persuade societies
and banks to take a more positive approach. It is, however, obviously
much more problematic to monitor activity in the private sector when it
does not have to be channelled through the local authority, as support
lending does.

The problems facing a local authority which wishes to improve levels
of conventional lending in its inner areas are, first, to persuade
building societies and banks to give it the necessary information to
produce a co-ordinated strategy and second, to get building societies
and banks to accept a co-ordinated strategy. Many building societies
and banks may consider it a waste of effort or not in their interest to
make information at such a detailed local level (potentially) available
to competitors. For the reality is that building societies are in
competition with each other and with banks for savers. Many also still
mistrust local authorities, particularly Labour authorities. There is
no legislation in this country similar to the US 'disclosure'
legislation, so a local authority wishing to obtain data and encourage
lending has no alternative but to rely on appeals to self-interest and
social responsibility and to attempt to persuade the building societies
that inner city lending is not too risky. Thus local authorities can
try to encourage building societies to lend by committing themselves to
the renewal of particular areas (see below) or by safeguarding loans by
the use of their mortgage indemnity powers under Section 111 of the
Housing Act 1980. However, these initiatives rely for their success on
the belief that building societies do not lend in the inner city
because it is unacceptably risky. It can be argued however that though
the risk in the inner city is greater than in the suburbs, this is not
the cause of lack of investment. Rather, the cause is that suburban
lending is administratively cheaper and the suburbs produce more
savings. According to this line of argument, the problem is that
suburban housing provides a sufficient outlet for all the funds
available. Unless investment in inner city housing can be made at
least as attractive as investment in the suburbs, guarantee schemes
will make little difference (assuming total funds are not increased).

The building societies argue that the Section 111 guarantees are very
cumbersome to operate and in this respect are inferior to their own
private sector insurance arrangements. They also argue that the latter
already cover them for any downmarket lending that they would ever be
willing to do. Below this, they say, the risks to buyers are too great
to warrant lending, even if the lenders risk nothing.

Obviously urban renewal schemes redress the balance of attractiveness
of inner cities a little but in cities like Liverpool and Birmingham
they are unlikely to produce the sort of London-style gentrification,
(or in US terminology 'displacement' of poorer people and blacks) which
would make inner cities attractive to lenders. In the USA, the need
for artificial incentives has been recognised by giving lending
institutions effectively a half of one per cent bonus on recognised
schemes for increasing lending in inner cities (Karn, 1980). We are
not proposing that such a thing is necessary or desirable here, or even
that it has proved effective in the USA. It is, however, useful to
recognise that in the USA it has been regarded as necessary to offer
financial incentives to conventional lenders to encourage them to lend
in the inner cities.

If the superior attractions of the suburbs and competition for funds have been the problems, it is not surprising that building societies have shown little interest in gathering information which identifies more clearly the scale of the unmet needs of the inner city. For a brief period around 1981-2 the intervention of the banks and the stagnation of the housing market seemed to be about to change this picture. Banks began to take such a large slice of the lending market that some building societies had to compete for borrowers. However, the banks' intervention declined in scale again. Since then the competition for savers has become the most significant feature of building society activity, and the savings coming into the societies have reached record levels.

This too should result in a relatively liberal approach to lending. But the experience of the earlier period of ample building society funds in 1972-74 suggests that without a fundamental change in building society policies and practices, even when funds are available a local authority will have a real problem in getting greatly increased building society investment in the inner city. Authorities will probably be able to negotiate a series of relatively small, special area initiatives to cover particular housing action areas, general improvement areas or, in Birmingham's case, enveloping schemes (see below). Alternatively a local authority's housing aid centre may make an arrangement to refer those with borrowing problems to particularly sympathetic building societies (e.g. Dudley's arrangements); or urban renewal teams may make arrangements with building societies about lending for improvement in particular housing action areas. Nevertheless, while all these initiatives are helpful to the areas or people concerned, if they are not accompanied by an increase in the resources devoted to inner city lending, they will merely result in one person or one area gaining conventional lending at the expense of another. As our survey shows, current levels of conventional lending are so low, even outside the housing action areas, that it will take much more than a few highly publicised special projects to give the inner city owner-occupied market greater stability and long-term security.

What could be done to bring about such a major switch? Somehow, ultimately, a local authority has to grapple with the problem that levels of inner city lending tend to be much lower than the statements of building societies would lead one to expect. Yet no one building society or bank bears responsibility for the lack of lending in a particular area, unless a commitment has been entered into for a special initiative. A logical ultimate aim of a local authority could then be to cover the entire inner city with 'special initiatives', so that if any area lacked lending some lending institution or group of institutions could be held responsible. This is the same 'area approach' to improving private investment for purchase as Birmingham originally had to urban renewal, namely that ultimately every aea which needed a policy initiative would be declared an HAA or GIA. That policy foundered on inadequate resources which led to too little activity in each area. It is the dilemma of the area approach to policy that if resources are limited, the policy fails, either because too few areas are treated and others suffer neglect relative to the ones where resources are concentrated, or because not enough is done in each of many areas. However, in theory, the position should be different over lending. The resources of the banks and building societies are immense. (Those of the pension funds if they could be enlisted are even greater). If banks, building societies and pension funds genuinely wish to help the inner city but need a structure within which to do so, a 'special initiative' approach with coverage of all those parts of the inner city which suffer lack of mortgage lending would be an obvious solution. Such measures might, however, be more applicable to areas with extremely low levels of lending (in our study, Soho or Saltley) or areas where there is already a dominant lender (e.g. Anfield or Sparkhill) than to raising levels of lending in areas with inadequate but not disastrously low levels of lending by a mix of societies (Handsworth).

We have outlined this approach, not because we expect it to happen readily or within the near future or because it is necessarily the best solution, but because it demonstrates the fundamental fact that there is much more to the support of inner city home ownership than the typical current type of 'initiative' which gives special help to certain housing action areas. The whole inner city home ownership market needs greater investment. If building societies and banks are really not prepared to commit themselves to adequate coverage, then the question of the future of low income inner city home ownership is brought into clear focus. If such commitment is not given and, if inner city home ownership is not to decline into an even more depressed state, the only practical policy is to allow the local authorities to lend. This could be done either by them borrowing from central government as they have done previously or by their receiving building society funds to lend on to individual buyers.

However even 'on lending' has been dismissed because it has been classed as 'public expenditure' and would hence be subject to the same government control. Nevertheless this approach retains quite wide support, even amongst building society officials. Many feel that it would be much more appropriate for the organisation responsible for policy concerning urban renewal and the 'life' of the inner city to also have responsibility for lending. Another argument is that the complications associated with 'searches', surveys and grants on inner city property make it more satisfactory that there is one agency through which all lending is channelled. This, it is argued, would avoid the current waste of time and money on multiple surveys of the same house by different lenders. Our survey also supports the view that, with local authority lending, vulnerable inner city buyers might be less likely to fall between the lending approaches of different branch managers and would have one clear source of loans.

Apart from a change in the Treasury definition of public expenditure, some changes would be required in local authority lending if this were to be a satisfactory solution. Loan processing would need to be much quicker and more attempts would have to be made to reach the bottom of the market. As we noted in Chapter 3, council lending has moved upmarket in the inner Birmingham areas from price levels at or below the survey area means during 1972/4 to above the means during 1975/9. In addition increases in council lending have been in the areas where there was also most building society lending. These results and the findings for Anfield over the shorter study period suggest that council lending is not always playing the role of lending of last resort, but is often slotting into the middle of the market.

One solution might be to target council lending more accurately by adopting a more active lending policy in certain areas or towards certain types of borrower instead of, as at present, setting maximum house price limits to lending and waiting for buyers to apply for loans. Such a 'targeting' or 'active' lending policy could be argued to ensure that council lending is directed to where it is most needed. This type of approach on an area basis has been adopted in Leeds, where lending has been heavily concentrated on the poorest areas of oldest housing, mostly HAAs. But, ironically, this has meant that buyers of the worst houses have had little trouble in raising loans, while those in slightly better property, with no local authority loans, have had difficulty because of the variable attitudes of building societies and their branches (Stevens et al 1982). Clearly there is a need for building societies and local authorities to co-operate to make their lending complementary, in whatever way best suits the local housing market, local institutions and local borrowers.

MANAGEMENT CONTROL AND MONITORING IN THE LENDING INSTITUTIONS

The study has shown important variations in the impact of branch lending practices. Yet individual savers have no idea of the variation between societies and branches in their attitudes to inner city lending and little opportunity to learn about it. Since membership and saving are essential prerequisites for entering the system, a commitment to a society and branch is generally made in advance of the loan application. Managers can be asked for advice about the sorts of lending the society is willing to do but again, in reality, the information given is usually so general as to be potentially misleading with regard to the specifics of any single case. Effectively a would-be borrower only learns such details when involved in an application to borrow on a specific house. They then have no opportunity to challenge the rules. More to the point for the potential borrower, building societies appear relatively uniform because managers tend to stress how normal their own procedures are. Little or no information is given which suggests societies differ in their practices.

This lack of specific information about lending practices is a conscious decision by societies. They argue, that because the situation is constantly changing, it is not possible to lay down guidelines for consumers which would be meaningful at any particular moment. But, in addition, societies have felt no need to compete over lending terms because of excess demand and this has diminished pressure on them to give much more specific guidance. As we have seen, this situation may be changing. Thirdly, societies want local managers to have discretion so that members are treated as individual cases; 'each case is treated on its merits' is the standard description. Much of this is very reasonable and in putting forward reforms one is conscious of these factors. However, the study indicates what variation there is in the treatment of similar cases. For instance, membership and savings requirements appeared to be waived for some but not others. The overall effect of this is to produce a very uneven pattern of lending by locality.

The term 'each case on its merits' is not an adequate criterion and there are strong grounds for suggesting that societies should narrow the boundaries for local managerial discretion. Although financial uncertainties will always remain, societies should be able to manage their finance in a sufficiently sophisticated way so that basic requirements can remain constant for reasonably long periods of time, e.g. minimum membership or minimum deposit. There seem few grounds for the constant change which appears to occur. A society should then develop a code of practice for branch managers regarding lending procedures and should monitor managers to ensure requirements are being met. In particular, monitoring should explore the degree to which requirements are waived for nominees from solicitors and estate agents, when ordinary individual savers are being turned away. The code of practice could be built up gradually, being refined in the light of the needs of both borrowers and lenders.

In drawing up this code, emphasis should be given to the reduction of uncertainty and the considerable variations in branch practice which this study and the CURS Monitoring Team study of Dudley (Housing Monitoring Team 1982) have demonstrated. In addition greater emphasis on training and education and professional qualifications through the Chartered Building Societies Institute may provide vehicles for informing practice. It is also possible that competition between societies for savings may force societies to specialise to a greater degree and to mark themselves out as more clearly different when attracting savers. Whether this will affect lending practices is uncertain but the effects of this trend must be considered, as must variations in the supply of mortgages relative to demand.

Our purpose here is not to formulate a model code or to try to press all building societies to adopt the same one, especially given the tensions surrounding this issue in the past (Boleat, 1979). Rather, we are suggesting that societies develop their own code as a basis for monitoring their managers' performance. At present they have inadequate management tools or criteria for measuring variations at the local level. To clarify policy and practice in this way would be in the interests of consumers and in the building societies' own interests in attracting future borrowers and hence savers, in having better management control and in identifying and targeting neglected markets. The clearing banks have recently adopted this approach in marketing their mortgage schemes, though the criteria have been rather 'restrictive'. Such codes could include a number of stipulations, such as that membership entitles savers to a loan subject to meeting certain guidelines. These guidelines could then be specified e.g. the condition of property, the income and age of the borrower, a minimum membership requirement or a minimum level of savings.

A second feature of such a code might be that members would be entitled to 'appeal' to head office if no satisfaction were obtained at the local level. This right and the procedures required should be clearly stated and its use encouraged. Thirdly, a code could state that, on being refused a loan, members should be entitled to a full explanation of the reasons and should be given suggestions as to how to proceed. Fourthly, the society could state publicly its minimum calculation regarding income requirements e.g. per cent of overtime, second earnings, etc. Fifthly, a code might state more precisely what the society's regulations about pre-1919 property were, so that investors could take this into consideration when opening an account. These are simply suggestions as to what areas might be considered.

With such publicly available codes of practice for each society, there would be increased competition to present attractions to borrowers instead of, as now, the publicity being mainly addressed to savers. The fear that codes might tend to become inflexible and act to the disbenefit of borrowers must be weighed against the present situation in which potential borrowers do not know lending criteria and flounder from one lender to another. Adverse publicity about inflexible lending practices would, in any case, probably tend to reduce the risk of harsh criteria. We believe that codes of practice might be more appropriate than regulations regarding mortgage disclosure. Evidence from the United States suggests that the information provided under these laws has not led to markedly different lending practices. Disclosure would be all the less effective here because few societies have a very local lending base and therefore it would be hard to determine which societies had a 'duty' to lend in a particular area and at what level. Organisations are complex phenomena responding to a variety of tensions and pressures. It is suggested that with closer internal supervision and control, societies could contribute more effectively to the buoyancy of inner city housing markets.

Besides these general features of management control and monitoring, there are some specific initiatives which might be, and which in some cases currently are being, adopted by building societies to help inner cities and ethnic minority savers and borrowers. Some of these are as follows:

a) Review of normal lending policies and procedures to examine in what ways these may be adversely affecting either inner cities or ethnic minorities; co-operation with the Commission for Racial Equality in the identification of problems.

b) Targeted marketing for ethnic minorities to provide foreign language material explaining lending terms, institutional arrangements and addressing issues of particular interest such as the ability to pay off a loan early.

c) Designation of staff with specific responsibility for certain 'inner city' tasks e.g. the co-ordination of lending activities with local authority plans for housing action areas; the maintenance, analysis and publication of data on lending in inner cities or to ethnic minorities; the stimulation of lending in inner cities.

d) Appointment of ethnic minority staff and use of ethnic minority agents. Building societies and banks should be encouraged to train and appoint as branch managers, surveyors and counter staff, people who belong to ethnic minority groups, and who could be placed in branches which are located in areas with a heavy preponderance of buyers from one or another ethnic minority. One midland building society in particular has deliberately approached the local Indian community to help it make appointments of Indians to branch offices, and we commend this successful initiative. A number of building societies are also building up links with Asian agents, which should in the long run increase levels of Asian borrowing from building societies (but see below).

The clearing banks already have very strong ties with the Asian communities, and there are many Asian agents who make referrals to the banks. This existing network of contacts could be used, if the banks so wished, to help Asians shift from short-term loans to conventional bank mortgages. Now that the banks have entered the conventional mortgage market, their activities in the inner city will have to be viewed in a different light. While they lent only short-term, it has on balance been a help to the inner city that they were willing to lend on types of property and to types of buyers whom other agencies were failing to consider. The fact that the loans were short-term and at higher interest rates was unfortunate but unavoidable, given the nature of their lending activity. Now, however, that nationally the banks are lending on conventional terms, one has to subject them to the same sorts of criticisms as building societies and ask whether they are going to provide conventional loans in the inner city. If they do, will it be on property which is as downmarket as that on which they currently lend, or will it, more probably, be similar to that mortgaged by building societies. Banks also need to be asked the same questions about the employment of ethnic minority staff and about the advice and help they give their borrowers about the claiming of tax relief on short-term loans.

AGENTS AND SOLICITORS

The role of middle-men in the inner city mortgage market emerges from our study as very important. They are very varied ranging from solicitors, estate agents, insurance agents and mortgage brokers to 'friends' or 'relations' who make introductions to banks or know someone in a building society. The banks particularly tend to expect a potential borrower who is not a customer to be 'introduced' by someone. Building societies, because of their dependence on agents and solicitors to channel savings to them, tend to give priority treatment to applicants sponsored by them.

Although it is clear from our study that using some intermediary of this sort is a very effective way of getting a loan, it is less clear that greater reliance on middle-men is a feature of the inner city loan market which we would want to see develop. One of the drawbacks of this system is that it is expensive in transaction costs for the buyer. Many agents who make introductions to banks and building societies charge substantial fees to the buyer. A number of the buyers we interviewed had to pay middle-men to get loans from the building society with which they saved. Surely the best solution for buyers is a more sympathetic response by building societies to direct approaches, not more use of expensive middle-men. There are particular dangers too for Asians who have language difficulties and who may be led to believe that they can obtain a loan only through an agent. Middle-men have an interest in building societies and banks making access to loans difficult for those who approach the lender directly.

We have to remember too that the evidence of situation tests by Political and Economic Planning (Daniel 1968; Smith 1977) is that estate agents themselves often discriminate on racial grounds. White agents, like the building societies, rarely employ ethnic minority staff, though there are growing numbers of Asian agents. The difficulty of regulating the real estate industry is probably an even more problematic one than that of changing building society allocation processes. Compulsory registration must be an important recommendation. But another recommendation, and probably just as important, is that the building societies and banks should be much more scrupulous about looking into the mode of operation of the agents with whom they deal, refusing to do business with those who make excessive charges or engage in other prejudicial activities.

PARALLELS WITH THE AMERICAN EXPERIENCE OF LOW INCOME HOME OWNERSHIP

From our survey, we can see that practices which make down market conventional lending easier are a necessary, but not a sufficient condition, for improving the owner-occupied stock and reducing longer-term problems to buyers. The fact is that by buying houses low income home owners are not ending their problems, and the worse the quality of their houses, the lower their incomes and the higher their repayments, the greater the long-term problems are. There is therefore nothing unreasonable about lenders taking precautions to see that the people they lend to will be able to sustain the ownership of their property, live in reasonable conditions and not neglect the property too much. The difficulty at present is to draw the line between what are reasonable precautions in the interests of lender and borrower alike and what amount to excuses for not lending in the inner city. It was apparent from our evidence of completely opposite decisions by different building societies about lending on the same property to the same buyer at the same time, that at present there is either no consensus about what constitutes a reasonable risk, or inner city lending is neglected for other reasons, notably that building societies have plenty of less problematic lending elsewhere.

While building societies err towards over-caution in the inner city, we have only to turn to the USA for evidence that just making lending easier does not solve the problems of low income home ownership (Karn, 1980; Karn 1982). After the 1968 riots in many American cities, the US government decided that the extension of home ownership to larger numbers of inner city blacks would create a greater sense of personal investment in neighbourhoods and hence reduce the likelihood of renewed violence. To this end the Federal Housing Administration (FHA) was required to direct its attention towards providing subsidies and guarantees for lending to lower income families, particularly in the inner city. Under the subsidised programme buyers were to pay 25 per cent of their income on the mortgage or a 1 per cent interest rate, whichever was the higher. The group of people who qualified for the subsidy were somewhat better off than public housing tenants or tenants of subsidised private rented properties but they were considerably poorer than the buyers who usually received mortgages guaranteed by the FHA. The unsubsidised 100 per cent guarantee schemes were also aimed at helping lower income buyers by encouraging institutions to lend in previously 'redlined' areas and by giving a 100 per cent loan covering all the costs, including fees. Despite all these incentives, the conventional lenders were still not interested and so the programmes had to rely on mortgage bankers (who are rather like mortgage brokers but who operate by initiating loans which they subsequently sell to the secondary mortgage market). The programme proved catastrophic and was abandoned. With no incentive to exercise caution on behalf of the investors since they were 100 per cent insured, the brokers lent on anything to anyone at inflated prices and then took little responsibility for helping those who found themselves in trouble. The result was a 2.0 per cent possession rate on the subsidised programme and a 2.4 per cent rate on the main unsubsidised scheme.

If we compare these FHA home ownership programmes with the US Department of Agriculture's Farmers' Homes programme for low income buyers we are immediately struck by the totally different emphasis and success rate. Farmers' Homes had the same subsidies as the discontinued FHA subsidy (Section 25) but was a direct government loan scheme. It was a 'supervised credit' system with heavy emphasis on local office contact with buyers, careful screening of applicants, and credit counselling to try to help people remain home owners as well as to buy initially. The effect of this was a low possession rate by American standards (about 0.4 per cent). However, the income level of borrowers began to drift up from the lower to the middle income bracket as the rising prices of second-hand houses and costs of construction, repairs, maintenance and services made it increasingly difficult for poorer people to meet the costs of owner occupation, even with a subsidy down to a 1 per cent interest rate on their mortgage.

To sum up these lessons from the USA, Farmers' Homes and low income FHA lending programmes present two sides of the same coin. Easy lending on cheap, deteriorated properties in poor, inner city environments did not make the properties intrinsically any better, nor did it increase the ability of the owners to improve them. All it did was give poor people heavily mortgaged ownership of an asset so dubious that no one else would buy it. Coupled with irresponsible lenders bearing no financial risk for mortgage failures, the programme produced massive default, homelessness and further damage to, and often destruction of, already poor properties.

The building societies, with their necessary stress on protecting the interests of investors would, like the savings and loan associations in the USA, never be likely to be lured into lending which risked default rates of this order. Their real concern for borrowers' interests and their own responsibility towards them would also make them unlikely to begin lending of this type, even if their investors were protected by government guarantees. Their cautious lending, like that of Farmers' Homes, results in the selection of the best properties, an inability to lend to the poorest, and a tendency for lending to creep upmarket as the costs of construction and maintenance increase. Many poorer people in the US cannot meet even the costs of maintaining their home, let alone purchasing it. At this point one is faced with the need for higher minimum incomes. Failing this, one has logically to press for a subsidy which includes the costs of maintenance and services as well as mortgage repayments. Attempts by Farmers' Homes to formulate such a subsidy for home owners have merely highlighted the greater ease of subsidising rented housing. How for instance does a government ensure that subsidies intended for maintenance and repairs are spent on them? Immediately we are faced with questions about the relationship between housing subsidies and income maintenance, about the conflicting interests of governments interested in the condition of the housing stock and low income people using their meagre resources as they see fit.

POLICY IMPLICATIONS FOR URBAN RENEWAL

Though buyers in our survey were spending large sums, for them, on maintenance and repairs, what they could actually achieve in this way were very marginal and probably only temporary improvements, relative to the actual physical defects in the property. Like the 1976 English House Condition Survey (Department of Environment, 1978), we found that improvements were often those which appealed most to occupiers but did little to improve the structure. This is perfectly rational behaviour on the part of the owners since it enhances the use-value and appearance of their property relatively cheaply. However, for the local authority, looking for fundamental structural rehabilitation to give its inner city housing a longer life, such expenditure is almost irrelevant. As the English House Condition Survey reported.

> much of this expenditure is incurred in decoration, minor repairs and 'cosmetic' improvements, and so perhaps no more than a half of this expenditure will have made a real or lasting contribution to improving the home.

Again like the English House Condition survey, we also found that improvements were least likely to have been made in the areas of poorest housing. This is to be expected because the poorest families buy the worst houses. Also it is rational behaviour on the part of the owners, who would have little chance of any return on their investment; but it is discouraging for a local authority seeking to renew its oldest stock.

In the context of the declining inner city rented housing stock in the USA, it is common to discuss the fact that, as areas decline, property passes into the hands of more and more 'marginal' owners who in order to make profits at all 'milk' the property of its remaining value. To do this they maximise rent income from the property whilst disinvesting by avoiding expenditure upon it such as maintenance, property taxes, mortgage payments, utility charges etc. Finally when no rent can be obtained they abandon it. One can see the role of the low income owners in parts of the inner city as being very similar, except that they are not so concerned with profit. The owner wishes to maximise the use of the property, and to minimise expenditure, for example, by avoiding long-term mortgages which involve interest payments on loans and by keeping repairs to essentials.

What we are seeing here is a fundamental conflict of interest between local authorities who are seeking to persuade inner city home owners to invest in improvements and the owners themselves who, though they may wish for better housing, either do not have the resources or are unwilling to invest more of their very limited budget and savings in housing as opposed to other items of expenditure. There is also the major problem for them of the 'valuation gap', the difference between what the house would sell for improved and what it would cost to purchase and improve.

These fundamental problems have retarded the progress of rehabilitation of owner-occupied housing. For instance in January 1982 in Liverpool's 37 declared housing action areas, there were 9,580 dwellings of which 5,742 were still in need of major works (i.e. either lacking at least one amenity, unfit or needing £2,000 or more spent in repairs). The renewal strategy for housing action areas in Liverpool has relied heavily on housing associations. In 1980/81 housing associations accounted for 57 per cent of renewal work in the city's housing action areas. However this strategy has helped only the rented sector. There have been no special policies to ensure improvement of owner-ocupied dwellings, other than the normal ones of enhanced levels of improvement grants in housing action areas and loans for improvement, despite the fact that in Anfield, for instance, owner-occupation accounted for 58 per cent of the stock in 1981.

In Birmingham the policy reactions have been rather different. In a city with a private rented sector much smaller than Liverpool's, housing association activity even if greatly enhanced could not have even the impact it has had there. In 1981, the proportions of private rented and housing association housing in Saltley, Soho, Sparkhill and Handsworth were, respectively, 14.5, 23.0, 24.8, and 28.9 per cent compared with 30.5 per cent in Anfield. Birmingham's reaction has been to adopt more positive policies towards the renewal of owner-occupied property.

Like Liverpool's, Birmingham's renewal task is massive. By 1978, 26 housing action areas had been declared but of the 8,480 privately-owned or rented properties scheduled for retention in them, only 506 had been improved. By 1980 some 10 per cent of the pre-1919 housing stock had been improved, leaving about 35 per cent substandard and most of the remainder rapidly becoming substandard. As a result, 1,390 compulsory purchase orders were made between 1978 and 1979. However, the council was reluctant to do more than use these as a threat because they did not want to enter a process that would ultimately lead to the wholesale conversion of owner-occupied and privately rented property in the inner city into housing association or local authority ownership. So instead of going ahead with compulsory purchase, to speed up improvements in housing action areas the city developed a new strategy termed 'enveloping'. This involves the council in carrying out a full external repair of a block of houses, with the owners' agreement. The cost of this policy is fairly high, on average £5,000 a house at 1981 prices for the exterior alone, but this is cheaper than the cost of repairs to a similar standard to individual dwellings in the same condition. It is of course dearer than 'patching repairs' done in the private sector but the end product is greatly superior - a secure structure instead of one that is rapidly becoming unfit through neglect.

So far enveloping has been able to make only a marginal impact on the problem of disrepair - only 2 per cent of the city's pre-1919 housing had been enveloped up to the middle of 1983. However, the visible impact of enveloping on the inner city is already great and Birmingham Council has decided to extend its enveloping activities in preference to adopting compulsory purchase orders and consequent municipalisation. Given central government encouragement the impact of this policy was all set to grow rapidly until subsequent public expenditure cuts intervened.

Enveloping or other smaller schemes of direct intervention such as improvement for sale or rent, need to be supplemented by the present system of improvement and repairs grants. These will continue to be necessary both for internal work on houses being enveloped and for the total improvement of other houses. Though grant arrangements were greatly improved in the 1980 Act, for them to be more effective and for take-up to be increased, they need to cover a greater percentage of the actual cost of improvement. At present the average costs have far outstripped approved costs so that even those with 90 per cent grants need to find a substantial sum themselves. Without this adjustment the grant system will not produce the results needed. If inner city home ownership is not to equate with inner city decay, the principle of public expenditure on privately-owned housing has to be accepted since lower income owners are incapable of being able to afford the kinds of repairs necessary to prevent further deterioration, let alone improve the stock.

Clearly enveloping has much to recommend it since by securing the external structure, it gives owners a breathing space before needing to tackle other improvements. It simultaneously allows them to concentrate their meagre resources on the interior improvements. As a result, and because of active local authority encouragement, the rate of internal improvements in Birmingham picked up. Enveloping also combines local authority control of standards of work with economies of scale and maximum environmental effects which result from improving whole blocks of houses at the same time. It has also increased the interest of reputable contractors in improvement work. However, enveloping is not suited to all locations and all property. It is particularly unsuited to improve scattered poor properties in an otherwise sound block, a situation typical of the upper end of the inner city housing market and of areas where there has been substantial housing association improvement activity.

The scale of the problem of disrepair is daunting in Liverpool and Birmingham. Birmingham Council has estimated, for instance, that it would require over £400 million over 10 years to improve the pre-1919 stock. The private sector has demonstrated that it is quite incapable of meeting this shortfall. This does not mean, however, that more could not be done by private lenders.

A greater proportion of improvement funds could come from building societies and banks but these loans would have to be in conjunction with grants to enable owners to take them up at all. In addition only a minority of existing buyers in the inner city have building society loans, and building societies are disbarred from giving loans for improvements to owners with an existing first mortgage from another source. A change may be needed in this rule if societies are to attempt to cover a greater proportion of loans for improvement in these areas. Even where building societies have expressed their willingness to lend for improvements to help meet the cost over and above grant expenditure, there are still problems. In particular, unemployed owners have found problems about obtaining such loans and this is an obstacle in housing action areas with high unemployment rates. In 1981 the unemployment rates in the study areas were as follows: Saltley 7.7 per cent, Soho 12.9 per cent, Sparkhill 8.0 per cent, Handsworth 13.0 per cent and Anfield 16.3 per cent (1981 Census, County Monitors). These levels have risen dramatically since.

Earlier in this concluding chapter, the suggestion was made that one way of trying to increase inner city lending would be to divide the inner city up into areas within which specific building societies had a commitment to lend. Taking the model of the American Neighbourhood Housing Services, it would also be possible, at the point at which people buy houses, to link improvement loans and grants into this network, preferably with technical help to owners about undertaking improvements. However the Neighbourhood Housing Services scheme makes it a condition of lending for purchase that people undertake improvements, with an additional loan, at the time of purchasing. The value to British inner cities of such an approach is, in our view, questionable. Given the low incomes and meagre savings of buyers and the worries that some already have about the level of their debt, a rigid policy of tying purchasers to large scale improvements at the initial stage would probably be counterproductive. A more phased approach might be more successful.

Another problem of adopting a structure similar to Neighbourhood Housing Services might be that it would create duplication of activities. In some local authorities urban renewal teams already carry out most of the improvement activities and advice covered by Neighbourhood Housing Services offices. For building societies to set up their own technical advice agencies would duplicate what currently happens. One expedient might be to set up some sort of urban renewal agency service funded for instance by the banks, building societies and the local authority jointly and independently staffed. In this way owners might have more reason to feel they were getting independent advice. Another approach adopted as an experiment in Sparkhill by the Financial Institutions Group entails building society officers spending two days a week in the local authority urban renewal office giving advice and assistance on borrowing.

The Financial Institutions Group scheme is only one of a host of joint initiatives between local authorities and lenders being tried throughout the country. Nevertheless the distance to be covered before building societies and banks reach the level of commitment required to undertake such initiatives on a large enough scale to make a real impact on the pre-1919 stock should not be underestimated. As we have seen in this study, they are not currently putting anywhere near enough resources into the purchase of houses, let alone their improvement. The 'enveloping' approach or any other policy for inner city renewal which retains home ownership as the major form of tenure, requires for its long-term success a steady flow of conventional, long-term building society (or bank) mortgages to finance sales. In Birmingham the building societies have declared their intention to lend in enveloped areas. If this does not actually occur, even after improvement properties will continue to be situated in a depressed market. If their owners have to rely on high interest, short-term loans with heavy monthly repayments they will continue to neglect the maintenance and repairs and the property will deteriorate again.

The picture of growing disrepair we have shown in our surveys of five inner areas merely serves to highlight the frightening picture of obsolescence and decay in the pre-1919 inner city stock in general. Lower income owners are inescapably both agents in this decline and sufferers from it. Growing disrepair at the lowest end of the market is, as we have seen, reflected in relatively falling prices, mortgaging problems and a further reluctance on the part of owners to 'send good money after bad'.

For renewal, the messages of this study are, _first_, that low income owner-occupation cannot be seen in itself as the mechanism through which major improvements can be brought about in the condition of the inner city stock; _second_, that thorough-going improvements, like enveloping, will require massive public or private investment and massive public subsidy, whatever the tenure of the properties; and _third_, that, without massive subsidies, there are fundamental conflicts of interest between on the one hand, local and central government which are interested in a sound housing stock with a good life-expectation and, on the other, owner-occupiers of poor property who want to live as cheaply as they can subject to certain expectations of privacy and amenities. The conflict of interest is brought out most clearly where the sensible public investment decision is demolition and new building and when the result of this for the owner is the loss of his cheap property.

Fear of demolition is also a source of conflict between local authorities and lenders. There is universal agreement that a regular programme of demolition is required but no one is facing up to the implications of this squarely; local authorities are reluctant to announce plans too far ahead or to let suspicions of demolition plans arise, since this blights the market in the eyes of lenders and buyers. But the practice of announcing demolition plans suddenly, as has been done recently in Saltley, is very threatening to those who have already bought, particularly recently. Officers and councillors are very conscious of the resistance of owner-occupiers to demolition and some even imply that demolition is no longer possible. This cannot however be the case, since the stock has to be renewed. The fundamental contradiction has to be faced that an owner-occupied market can only be sustained if lenders know the property will retain its value, yet both gradual deterioration of the existing stock and plans to demolish the worst stock threaten values. The relationship between building societies and local authorities is complicated by this contradiction. Building societies feel that vague local authority 'plans' tend to make markets depressed. Yet it is inevitable that a responsible local authority, aware of the need for systematic renewal of the stock, will have to make plans to demolish the worst property. On their side, local authorities feel that building societies undermine their renewal plans by being over-cautious about inner cities, yet they themselves have to admit that demolition will have to take place if renewal does not succeed. Contact between authorities and building societies has increased in recent years because they have had discussions about the support lending scheme and more recently about special initiatives on urban renewal but there will always be differences of interest between the lenders, the local authorities as planning and housing agencies, and the inner city buyers themselves. This point must be considered if experiments such as 'joint renewal agencies' are to be tried (see Housing Monitoring Team, 1978 for building society views).

PROSPECT AND RETROSPECT

Our discussion of the arenas for policy development regarding low income inner city home ownership must be placed in the context of housing policy and housing provision as a whole. As we stated at the outset, underlying this specific piece of research is a general concern with the intersection between low incomes and poor housing. It is significant that although we have witnessed the implementation of an array of new policy initiatives over the last decade there is little in our findings which gives cause for optimism nor to suggest that the conclusions to the previous study are in any way now invalid. As was stated with respect to that study:

> Because of the financial difficulties of inner city owner-occupiers, the switch from private unfurnished renting to owner-occupation in the inner city has not, in many respects, conferred the benefits on owners which many proponents of owner-occupation might have expected. The houses in these areas are still of poor quality. They still need improvement and repairs but owners are often unable to afford to carry them out, even with grant aid. Though owners may be said to be accumulating a capital asset, and are certainly attracted to owner-occupation by this, doubts as to whether house values will be maintained, in the absence of conventional mortgages and with the introduction of improvement policies, also lead to doubts as to the security of the investment.

> Government policies for the inner cities seem consistently to ignore the inescapable fact that the incomes of the residents are too low to meet the cost of better housing. This fact does not disappear if one introduces improvement rather than new building and current grant levels do not fill the gap. Similarly greater availability of mortgages in inner areas will not meet this problem, in the absence of an increase in the supply of cheap housing. There is no solution to inner city housing problems which is not enormously costly. (Karn, 1979).

In many respects these conclusions are even more pertinent today than they were in 1975. Predictably, inner city housing has responded to market forces with increasing stratification and with the emergence of a sump of housing, rapidly deteriorating, increasingly difficult to finance, falling in relative price position and occupied by households with limited resources to improve. With increasing unemployment and general economic stress in these areas, the fact that low income home owners receive very little subsidy compared with high income owners becomes a more and more glaring anomaly of housing and public expenditure policy. Government initiatives to give special help to certain groups of buyers have not altered this. They have merely introduced 'horizontal inequity' as well as 'vertical inequity'. It is interesting to compare the incomes of the buyers in this survey with those of people in the present government's special low cost home ownership initiatives (since the latter have been judged to deserve special help). It can be shown that the buyers in this survey had incomes if anything slightly lower than the people buying houses under the Purchase and Improve (PIMS) scheme in Birmingham, and very considerably lower than those of people buying council houses with a local authority mortgage (for an assessment of low income home ownership initiatives see Forrest, Lansley and Murie, 1984). The income ranges of the poorest people buying 'build for sale' properties in the inner city started above the level at which the incomes of the most affluent of the surveyed buyers finished. Yet all these schemes give special subsidies through selling houses at prices which either give a discount (council house sales) or which write off part of the cost of improvement (PIMS) or land (Build for Sale). The fact that the buyers in our survey had lower incomes but very little subsidy raises questions of the 'equity' of special schemes, as between one group of low or moderate income buyers and another.

The future for owner-occupied housing in these inner city areas is therefore bleak. It would appear that without very heavy public investment in these areas on the scale of a vastly larger version of Birmingham's enveloping schemes they are likely to continue to decline. The American experience of the untrammelled working of market forces suggests that a new generation of slums may be in the making. We could even experience the same wholesale abandonment or dereliction of owner-occupied housing as found in inner areas of US cities, especially if prices begin to fall in absolute as well as relative terms in response to increasing fabric deterioration and the inability to raise a mortgage or find a buyer. Ultimately, a choice has to be made between this type of urban decay leading to the need for a new round of slum clearance before the end of the century or immediate investment of substantial public and private funds for renewal and mortgage finance. In addition, if government policy is to retain or expand the present level of home ownership of the pre-1919 stock and to expand home ownership more generally amongst low income groups, then it is clear that some kind of extensive and heavy subsidisation of lower income owner-occupiers will be necessary. This will be essential first, to enable them to improve their properties, second, to enable them to continue to maintain them, and third, to enable subsequent lower income purchasers to be able to afford to buy the improved houses.

Appendix

Appendix I
Research methods

The surveys which were carried out during the course of this project were the recent buyers surveys, the reinterview survey and the house condition survey.

1. The recent buyers surveys

The bulk of resources devoted to the project have been allocated to the recent buyers surveys in Birmingham and Liverpool. In the case of Birmingham, three of the four areas surveyed had been previously surveyed in 1974, and it was essentially as a follow-up to the 1974 survey that the 1979 recent buyers surveys were conceived. The longitudinal nature of the project has therefore meant that the methodology used in the 1979 recent buyer surveys has replicated that used in 1974 in order to make the results comparable. The methodological problems involved in both the 1974 and 1979 recent buyers surveys can be divided into two parts: the nature of the population to be taken as the basis from which the sample is drawn, and the type of sampling method to use. We consider these in turn.

(a) The population : the survey areas in 1974

The study of inner city home ownership immediately raises the question of what is meant by the 'inner city'. Unfortunately there is no general agreement on a definition, and in terms of housing the nearest approximation has been to equate the inner city areas with areas where pre-1919 housing predominates or where such stock has been cleared and replaced, usually with post-war local authority housing. This was the definition used in the 1974 Birmingham survey, and as far as owner occupation goes, the overwhelming bulk of inner city home ownership is found in pre-1919 housing (as against renewal areas) in the inner ring of the city.

Strictly speaking, in order to be able to generalise about inner city home ownership in Birmingham, using the above definition, it would be necessary to conduct a random sample of recent buyers of pre-1919 housing. A sample drawn from this population would be scattered randomly around the whole inner ring of the city. However, the 1974 survey of recent buyers funded by the Social Science Research Council was designed as three discrete area surveys within inner Birmingham. While this meant that the degree to which it has been possible to generalise about 'inner Birmingham' is somewhat reduced, the problem is lessened by the fact that the areas are relatively large. The four

areas ultimately surveyed in Birmingham in 1979 comprise some 13,000
dwellings: about one-fifth of the pre-1919 inner ring housing stock.
Because of this, the data is more reliable as a guide to the nature of
inner city home ownership than if only one or two small areas were
surveyed. In addition, area surveys in themselves have important
advantages. First, the study of discrete areas provides a wealth of
additional data, particularly on movement into and out of the areas and
on local housing markets and conditions. Second, and perhaps decisive
in 1974, was the fact that given the heavy concentrations of New
Commonwealth and Pakistan immigrants in inner Birmingham, areas could
be chosen in such a way as to maximise the diversity of ethnic groups:
English, Irish, Indians, Pakistanis and West Indians in particular.
Working on 1971 Census data and on local information, Sparkhill was
chosen because it was a largely white area, Soho was a mixed Indian and
West Indian area and Saltley a mixed white and Pakistani area. Since
1974 there have been further increases in the number of ethnic minority
purchasers changing the characteristics of these areas somewhat, and,
according to the results of the 1979 surveys and 1981 Census, further
changes are still taking place. The 1974 survey confirmed that there
were major differences between different ethnic groups concerning
the nature of owner-occupation and its social and economic
arrangements, and it is now clear that ethnic difference is one of the
most important variables in understanding inner city owner-occupation.

Finally, there was one other important factor which determined the
nature of the survey areas chosen. The quality of the pre-1919 housing
stock varies considerably. Some housing is in a good state of repair,
improved and being bought by higher income earners. In particular,
outlying parts of the pre-1919 stock, notably in Harborne and Kings
Heath appear to be undergoing a process of gentrification at least on a
small scale. Owner-occupation in such areas is less likely to involve
either problems of poor maintenance or difficulty in obtaining
conventional building society finance. On the other hand, there are
some areas, often on the edge of clearance areas, which are in such a
poor condition that building societies would not consider providing
mortgages on them. Since one of the main concerns in the project was
the problem of financing marginal housing with building society loans,
an important consideration was to survey areas where the housing stock
was 'marginal': neither completely unproblematic nor impossible to
finance. The survey areas were therefore delineated in such a way as
to include mostly housing which would be eligible for consideration by
building societies but which would be marginal for building societies
to finance. Such areas would be most likely to be made up of housing
on which there would be some building society finance as well as bank,
finance company, and other non-conventional finance.

Summing up, then, the main criteria in selecting the three original
survey areas in 1974 were (1) the age of the housing; (2) the ethnic
composition of the buyers and (3) the likelihood of building society
finance. One additional criterion was that there should be a
sufficiently high percentage of owner-occupation in the areas so that
locating recent buyers among tenants would not entail too much wasteful
sifting. In the event, the three criteria above proved sufficient in
combination to ensure that the home ownership rate in those areas was
around 50 per cent. (According to the 1981 Census the proportions of
home ownership in the wards within which the survey areas were located

were as follows: Saltley 50 per cent, Handsworth 53 per cent, Anfield 58 per cent, Soho 62 per cent and Sparkhill 65 per cent).

The actual selection of the survey areas and the delineation of the survey area boundaries were carried out by examination of the census and other survey data available at the time. In 1974, the 1971 Census was the most useful source, and the survey areas were initially delineated by choosing a number of coterminous enumeration districts which as closely as possible conformed to the required criteria. The survey areas so delineated were made up of between 2,000 and 4,000 dwellings, which, given a home ownership rate of about 50 per cent, would, it was hoped, generate at least 100 interviews with recent buyers. (Details of the sampling are given below). In the case of Saltley, it was decided to select the enumeration districts comprising the Community Development Project (CDP) area because the initial survey was conducted in collaboration with the CDP. In addition the wealth of data which the CDP had generated in the Saltley survey area was available for helping to estimate the size of the owner-occupied market and was particularly useful for estimating how large a sample of households would be needed to obtain the right number of interviews.

(b) The Sampling Technique

The recent buyers surveys in both 1974 and 1979 involved interviewing a number of owner-occupiers who had purchased their houses within a defined period of being interviewed. No official records or sources existed from which to identify recent buyers as against longer established buyers, or even to identify owner-occupiers as against households in other tenures. It was therefore impossible to sample recent buyers directly from a known finite population of recent buyers, or even from a known finite population of owner-occupiers. Instead, it was necessary to draw a sample from a population of residential addresses in the survey areas and then to conduct a door to door 'sift survey' to distinguish owner-occupiers from other tenures and, having done this, to distinguish recent buyers from longer-established owner occupiers. These recent buyers were then asked for an interview. Obtaining such a sample involved considerable effort on the part of interviewers. They had to visit a large number of houses in order to obtain a relatively small number of eligible households, not all of whom were available for interview or were willing to be interviewed.

The sample of addresses given to the interviewers was drawn from the rating register. Using information in the rate books, we were able to eliminate local authority and housing association tenancies and properties used entirely for business purposes. It was not, however, possible to distinguish reliably between owner-occupiers and private tenants. Indeed, with the rapid conversion of private tenancies into owner-occupation, and the time-lag before rating books are up-dated, we would probably have had to include private tenancies in our sample in any case. The resulting list of sampled addresses therefore included all fully or partially residential property where the ratepayer was either a private landlord or tenant or an owner-occupier. This list therefore included two major categories of household which were not wanted: (a) private tenants and (b) owner-occupiers who were not recent buyers. These were eliminated at the 'sift survey' stage, by asking sampled households whether they were an owner-occupier and, if so, when they bought their house.

To sum up, a number of different factors influenced the size of the sample needed.

(a) the size of the survey area and the number of residential addresses within it.

(b) the home ownership rate, and so the number of owner-occupiers in the area.

(c) the number of recent buyers in the residential population, which is a function of the turnover of the owner-occupied housing stock in terms of house sales, together with the rate at which landlords sell rented houses into owner-occupation either to sitting tenants or with vacant possession.

(d) how narrowly 'recent' buyers are defined as distinct from longer-established owner-occupiers. Clearly, if recent buyers are defined as those who have bought in the last twelve months, the number of recent buyers in a survey area will be smaller than if they are defined as those who have bought over the last five years.

(e) the number of interviews required, and the response rate.

Given the nature of the survey areas in terms of home ownership rate and the likely rate of turnover of the owner-occupied stock the only variables which could be controlled by the researchers were the size of the survey area, the definition of a 'recent buyer', and the size of the sample. In practice, all three of these variables were changed over the course of the two sets of surveys.

(c) The 1979 recent buyers surveys : changes and additions

Though the sampling technique remained the same there were four main differences between the 1979 and 1974 recent buyers surveys: the questionnaire was substantially revised: the size of the sample in each area was increased from just over 100 interviews to around 150 to facilitate a more detailed analysis of specific variables; two new areas, Handsworth in Birmingham and Anfield in Liverpool, were added, to give better comparative data on West Indian and white inner city buyers; and the definition of 'recent buyers' was broadened to include more years. The latter change was made in order to get continuity with the 1972-4 study. Extending the definition of recent buyer from 3 to 4.5 years extended the date of purchase of the earliest buyers in the 1979 surveys back to January 1975, the latest date at which any of the 1974 survey sample had purchased. Thus by combining the 1974 and 1979 survey results, a sample of buyers was generated for each year from January 1972 to August 1979.

In the smallest area, Sparkhill, an extension was added to the 1974 area. In 1974, Sparkhill still had a majority of white buyers, but already various groups of Asians were buying there. Initial results from the 1979 survey suggested that Sparkhill was rapidly becoming increasingly Asian, yet Sparkhill was the only one of our Birmingham survey areas with any number of white buyers. It had initially been hoped to survey an inner area of Birmingham where whites were the predominant buyers, but this had to be abandoned because it emerged that there was no sufficiently large area with such a characteristic. In the light of these facts it was decided that if an extension were needed to Sparkhill it should be done by extending to an area where the number of white buyers would be maximised. A number of enumeration districts to the south-west of the survey area were therefore identified as being the best extension. In the event only two streets were released to supplement the original survey area before sufficient interviews were obtained. In any case Asian buyers appeared in these streets as well.

(d) The Handsworth recent buyers survey

As we said earlier, one of the areas surveyed in 1974, Soho, was chosen primarily because it was known to have high concentrations of West Indians at the time of the 1971 Census. Enumeration district data for the survey area showed that 16.5 per cent of the population were West Indian in origin. This ethnic group was of particular interest because West Indians were among the earliest of the post-war immigrants from the New Commonwealth. In addition, there was some evidence, subsequently supported by other surveys, that the housing situation of West Indians differed considerably from that of the more recent Asian immigrants.

The 1974 survey of Soho, then, had as one of its main aims the collection of data on recent West Indian buyers to compare them with other ethnic groups. However, the results of the 1974 survey showed that although, as already indicated, West Indians made up 16.5 per cent of the survey area's population, only 14 per cent of recent buyers were West Indians. Since only 104 interviews were obtained in this area, and since the number of West Indian recent buyers in the other two survey areas was negligible, the total number of West Indian buyers interviewed in the three areas was insufficient to enable detailed comparisons to be made with other ethnic groups.

The results of the 1979 re-survey were even more disappointing in relation to the numbers of West Indian buyers, because the percentage of recent West Indian buyers in Soho fell from 14 per cent in 1974 to only 7 per cent in 1979 out of a total of 170 interviews. This in turn made it more important to identify a new survey area in which West Indians were buying in considerable numbers.

The considerable decline in the number of West Indian recent buyers in Soho between 1974 and 1979 raised important questions about the tenure and residential location of West Indians in Birmingham. A number of possibilities presented themselves by way of explanation of what was happening. One possibility was that West Indians were buying in specific areas of inner Birmingham not yet surveyed. If this were so then the extra area to be surveyed would enable us to identify locational factors among West Indian owner-occupiers. Another possibility was that West Indians were dispersing more widely in the Birmingham area. If this were so then we would be unable to identify an inner area of West Indian buyers, and this fact would be at least indirect evidence in support of that explanation. A third possibility was that the tenure patterns of West Indians were changing. Unpublished Birmingham data from the 1977 National Dwellings and Housing Survey suggested this was happening, with larger numbers of West Indians entering council housing and housing associations. This would imply that a declining home ownership rate was taking place among second generation West Indians.

The identification of an area where West Indians were buying proved to be difficult. Extensive enquiries were made with estate agents, local West Indian community workers, housing associations, urban renewal teams, and others in an attempt to identify an area where West Indians were buying in considerable numbers. It became clear that West Indians were not buying in large numbers anywhere, but there was considerable agreement among those from whom we enquired that an area in Handsworth bisected by the Perry Barr Expressway, including Birchfield, and bounded by Wellington Road, Lozells Road, Aston Road and Witton Road was the most likely place to find concentrations of West Indian recent buyers. This area was at the outer limit of the contiguous pre-1919 housing stock. Indeed, parts of the area, particularly east of the Expressway, included a considerable number of early inter-war houses.

This area was chosen for survey and was named 'Handsworth'. At this stage there was still considerable uncertainty as to how many West Indian buyers we would find. We therefore decided to sample the area in an identical manner to the original survey areas but to monitor closely the proportion of West Indians being interviewed. In addition, the sift sheets were altered to provide us with additional information concerning the ethnic origin as well as the tenure of non-eligible households. Information was also collected on West Indian owner occupiers who were ineligible for interview because they had bought before 1975, so we would have a disaggregation showing how many ineligible West Indian owner-occupiers bought in different years.

Once the Handsworth survey was under way it became apparent that though there were more West Indian recent buyers than in Soho, they still represented only a moderate minority of recent buyers; out of 132 interviews obtained, 20.5 per cent were West Indian. This was considerably more than obtained in Soho even in the 1974 survey (14 per cent). It was also more than the percentage of total West Indian households in the survey area according to 1971 Census enumeration district data (13.7 per cent). It was therefore clear that considerable numbers of West Indians were buying in the Handsworth survey area, though the area could by no means be described as an area where West Indians were the predominant buying group in the way that Soho or Saltley could be described as areas in which Indians or Pakistanis were the predominant buying groups.

The Anfield (Liverpool) recent buyers survey

The Anfield survey was chosen in consultation with the Liverpool City Planning Department which delineated an approximate area of pre-1919 housing where British or Irish born buyers predominated and where the home ownership rate was over 30 per cent. Further analysis of existing data and windscreen and walking surveys, established a large area immediately south of the Anfield Football Ground, including a number of housing action areas. The area chosen was considerably larger than those in Birmingham since we were unsure what the turnover rate would be. Our experience had been limited to ethnically diverse areas in Birmingham and so in case the ratio of recent to longer-established buyers was much lower in Anfield than in Birmingham, we delineated a larger area than we thought we would need in order to ensure that we obtained around 200 interviews.

Because of this, a slightly different sift procedure was used in Anfield. Streets were released in small area batches for sifting and interviewing, beginning in the north around the football ground and working gradually south and south east. When sufficient interviews had been obtained, no further batches were released and a discrete survey area was thereby defined.

One further point needs to be made about the Anfield sampling procedure. Interviewing was carried out in the Autumn of 1980 and it was found that the response rate in the streets adjacent to the football ground was lower than in the rest of the survey area, because many households were refusing to answer the door after dark or on days when matches were being played. To boost the response rate it was therefore decided that addresses where no response was obtained would be revisited in the summer of 1981, after the end of the football season. However, the riots which took place in Liverpool in May 1981 forced us reluctantly to abandon that attempt. As a result, as can be seen from the sample results (Table 1), the response rate in Anfield is somewhat lower than in Birmingham, though still well within the bounds of acceptability.

2. The 1980 reinterview survey

The purpose of this survey was to re-contact as many as possible of the households interviewed in the 1974 recent buyers survey of Saltley, Soho and Sparkhill in order to discover how their situation had changed over the six to eight years since buying. The response rate of the re-interview survey is shown in Table 2.

3. The 1981 House Condition Survey

A one in five systematic sub-sample was taken from the recent buyers interviewed in the four Birmingham areas in 1979. A schedule was drawn up designed to be comparable with that of the English House Condition Surveys of 1976 and 1981, and applied by a qualified Public Health Officer. A total of 130 dwellings were sampled. In addition, about half a dozen of the buyers in the sub-sample were interviewed about repairs, repair activities and the effect of house condition on household finances, relationships and other domestic and household factors.

Appendix Table A.1
Sampling Results, 1979 Recent Buyers Survey

Households	Saltley	Soho	Sparkhill	Handsworth	Anfield
Total sampled	1098	1114	1084	1139	1577
of which	(1 in 3)	(1 in 2)	(1 in 2)	(1 in 3)	(1 in 3)
(a) owner-occupied	676	750	663	619	766
(b) privately rented	203	160	285	178	518
(c) local authority	24	41	13	11	-
(d) housing assoc.	103	80	27	229	38
(e) other (incl. empty)	54	83	5	52	136
(f) refusals	4	8	16	3	15
(g) no contact made	34	17	12	47	104
Owner-occupiers sampled	676	750	663	619	766
of which					
(a) bought before 1975	433	496	534	448	462
(b) inherited	8	15	18	17	25
Eligible for interview					
of which					
(a) interviewed	168	170	154	130	213
(b) refused or head of household away	5	6	6	24	66
Response rate (%)	97.0	96.5	96.1	84.4	76.3[1]

(1) The lower response rate in Anfield was due primarily to a reluctance by many households living near Liverpool Football Ground to answer their doors, first during interviewing in the football season 1980/81 and then during subsequent attempts to recontact in summer 1981 after the riots.

Source: Survey

Appendix Table A.2
Response Rate to the Reinterview Survey 1980

	Saltley	Soho	Sparkhill
completed interviews	60	57	53
household moved away	44	27	38
property empty or demolished	6	7	3
owner abroad	-	2	2
property empty pending modernisation	4	-	-
original buyer resident but is now tenant	2	2	-
refused, not contacted	3	9	5
Total	119	104	101
response rate (%)	50	55	53

Source: Survey

Appendix Table A.3
Home Ownership Levels in Special Areas, 1981

(Areas designated under the Inner Urban Areas (Special Area) Orders under the 1978 Inner Urban Areas Act)

Special Area Wards within:-	Percentage of Home-ownership, 1981
	%
Hackney	16.5
Islington	16.9
Lambeth	26.6
Docklands	
Greenwich	20.7
Lewisham	15.0
Newham	21.5
Southwark	6.0
Tower Hamlets	4.6
Manchester	34.7
Salford	22.0
Liverpool	39.2
Gateshead	32.6
Newcastle-on-Tyne	38.4
Birmingham	50.5

Source: 1981 Census

Appendix Table A.4
Special Area Wards with 40% or more Home Ownership

		%			%
Hackney:	Homerton	42.6	Newcastle:	Gosforth No 1	58.9
Lambeth:	Knight's Hill	41.9		Gosforth No 2	57.0
	St Leonards	40.9		Newburn No 1	43.0
	Streatham Sth	69.4		Newburn No 2	42.7
	Thurloe Park	48.0		Newburn No 3	66.4
Docklands:	Charleton	40.3		Dene	62.1
Manchester:	Alexandra	57.3		Fawdon	40.9
	Bradford	40.4		Fenham	61.5
	Cheetham	47.1		Heaton	52.6
	Gorton Nth	53.5		Jesmond	55.5
	Gorton Sth	41.0		Walkergate	55.1
	Levenshulme	61.6		Wingrove	51.2
	Lightbowe	58.3	Birmingham:	Acocks Green	61.1
	Longsight	46.6		Billesley	49.2
	Rusholme	44.7		Brandwood	52.6
Salford:	Langworthy and			Erdington	43.5
	Seedly	44.5		Gravelly Hill	52.8
Liverpool:	Aigbarth	50.5		Hall Green	78.0
	Anfield	58.1		Handsworth	52.8
	Arundel	40.1		Harborne	57.8
	County	43.1		Moseley	53.8
	Dingle	43.2		Oscott	73.3
	Grassendale	78.4		Perry Barr	86.0
	Kensington	42.1		Rotton Park	41.8
	Old Swan	57.6		Saltley	50.2
	Picton	57.8		Sandwell	72.4
	Tuebrook	49.1		Shard End	43.7
	Warbreck	64.6		Sheldon	57.1
				Small Heath	58.7
Gateshead:	No 4	50.5		Soho	62.1
	No 5	69.8		Sparkbrook	42.2
	No 6	42.6		Sparkhill	65.0
	No 7	41.0		Stockland Green	48.4
	No 10	48.6		Washwood Heath	52.2
	No 19	51.8		Yardley	59.1
	No 20	45.7			
	No 22	46.7			

Bibliography

Anderson, J. et.al, Redundant Spaces, Academic Press, London 1983.

Bassett, K. and Short, J., Housing and Residential Structure, Routledge and Kegan Paul, London 1980 (a).

Bassett, K. and Short, J., 'Patterns of building society and local authority lending in the 1970s', Environment and Planning A, Vol 12, 1980 (b), p.279-300.

Bell, C., Vacant dwellings in the private sector - a case study of the City of Birmingham. Unpublished M.Soc.Sci Thesis in Urban and Regional Studies, University of Birmingham, 1976.

Benwell Community Development Project, Private Housing and the Working Class, Benwell Community Project, Final Report Series No. 3, Newcastle 1978.

Boddy, M., 'The structure of mortgage finance : building societies and the British social formation'. Transactions of the Institution of British Geographers. New Series, Vol. 1, No. 1, pp. 58-73, 1976.

Boddy, M., The Building Societies, Macmillan, London 1980.

Boddy, M. and Gray, F., Filtering theory and the legitimation of inequality. Policy and Politics Vol. 7, No. 1, 39-54, 1979

Boleat, M., The Building Societies Association, The Building Societies Association, London 1979.

Bowmaker, E., The Housing of the Working Classes, London 1895.

Bridges, L., 'Keeping the lid on: British urban social policy 1975-81' Race and Class, XXIII, 2/3 pp. 171-185.

Burney, E., Housing on Trial; a study of immigrants and local government. Institute of Race Relations, London 1967.

Byrom, R., 'The Building Society Valuer', Estates Gazette, London 1979.

City of Plymouth, Report on Support Lending to Finance Committee by the City Treasurer, Plymouth 1981.

Cole, G., Building Societies and the Housing Problem, Design for Britain Series 28, Co-operative Permanent Building Society, London 1943.

Crook, A.D.H. and Bryant, C.L., Local authorities and private landlords: a case study of the impact of changes in the private rented sector on inner city housing, Sheffield Centre for Environmental Research, Sheffield University 1982.

Dahya, B., 'Pakistani Ethnicity in Industrial Cities in Britain in A. Cohen (ed.)' Urban Ethnicity, Tavistock, London 1974.

Daniel, W., Racial Discrimination in England, Penguin Books 1968.

Department of Employment, Family Expenditure Survey, HMSO, London 1980.

Department of Environment, Housing Policy, HMSO, London 1977.

Department of Environment, English House Condition Survey, 1976, HMSO, London 1978.

Department of Environment, English House Condition Survey, 1981, HMSO, London 1983.

Doling, J. and Williams, P., 'Building Societies and Local Lending Behaviour', Environment and Planning A, Vol. 15, 1983 p. 663-673.

Duncan, S., 'Self-help; the allocation of mortgages and the formation of housing sub-markets', Area. Vol. 8, No. 4, 1977, pp. 302-316.

Dunleavy, P., Urban Political Analysis, Macmillan, London 1980.

Dunleavy, P., The Politics of Mass Housing, Clarendon Press, Oxford 1981.

Edwards, T., Building for Sale and Improving for Sale in Inner Birmingham. Unpublished paper to PTRC Conference, July 1982.

Elliott, B. and McCrone, D., The City: Patterns of Domination and Conflict, Macmillan, London 1982.

Fenton, M., 1977, 'Asian Households in Owner-Occupation' Working Papers on Ethnic Relations No. 2, SSRC Research Unit on Ethnic Relations, 1977.

Flett, H., 'Black Council Tenants in Birmingham', Working Papers on Ethnic Relations, No. 12, SSRC Research Unit in Ethnic Relations, 1979.

Forrest, R. et.al., The Inner City: In Search of the Problem Geoforum, 10, 1980, pp. 109-116.

Forrest, R., Lansley, S. and Murie, A. A Foot on the Ladder: An evaluation of low cost home ownership initiatives, Working Paper No. 41, SAVS, University of Bristol 1984.

Friend, A., 'Failed Strategies, Falling Investment, Liverpool's Housing Programme and Government Policy', CHAS Occasional Paper No. 6, Catholic Housing Aid Society, London 1981.

Gibson, M. and Langstaff, M., An Introduction to Urban Renewal Hutchinson, London 1982.

Greater London Council, Greater London House Condition Survey, Greater London Council, London 1981.

Grime, K. and Smith, C., 'Mortgage allocation in Salford and Manchester, Area', 14: 305-312, 1982.

Grosskurth, A., 'Toothless Watchdog' Roof (2) 19, 1983, pp. 19-24.

Guardian, the 21 Jan. 1984.

Hall, P., (ed.), The Inner City in Context, Heinemann, London 1981.

Harrison, M., 'Risk capital, equal opportunity and urban issues' Environment and Planning A, Vol. 11, 1979 pp. 585-596.

Harrison, M. & Stevens, L., 'Ethnic Minorities and the Availability of Mortgages', Research Memorandum 5, Dept. of Social Policy, Leeds University 1982.

Hebbert, M., The Inner City Problem in Historical Context, SSRC Inner City in Context Paper 5, Social Science Research Council 1981.

Henderson, J. and Karn, V., 'Race, Class and the Allocation of Public Housing', Urban Studies, Vol. 21, May 1984.

Housing Monitoring Team, 'Building Societies, a Head Office View'. Research Memorandum 64, C.U.R.S. University of Birmingham 1978.

Housing Monitoring Team, 'Building Societies and the Local Housing Market', Research Memorandum 90, C.U.R.S. University of Birmingham 1982.

Karn, V., 'Property Values Amongst Indians and Pakistanis in a Yorkshire Town', Race Volume X, 3, 1969, pp. 269-284.

Karn, V., The Operation of the Housing Market in Immigrant Areas. Final Report to the SSRC, (unpublished) 1976.

Karn, V., 'The Impact of Housing Finance on low income Owner-Occupiers' Working Paper, 55, C.U.R.S., University of Birmingham 1977.

Karn, V., The Financing of Owner-Occupation and its impact on Ethnic Minorities, New Community, Winter 1977/8 pp. 49-63.

Karn, V., 'Low Income Owner-Occupation in the Inner City', in C. Jones, (ed.) Urban Deprivation and the Inner City, Croom Helm, London 1979.

Karn, V., The Position of Lower Income Households in the Owner-Occupied Housing Market in the USA and Great Britain, Urban Institute, Washington DC, 1980.

Karn, V., 'Private Housing at All Costs: Some Lessons from America in J. English (ed.)' The Future of Council Housing, Croom Helm, London 1982.

Karn, V., Research on Housing and Race in Britain: Current Themes and Future Priorities SSRC, London 1983.

Karn, V., 'Arrears', Roof Jan - Feb 1983 pp. 11-14.

Kemeny, J., The Myth of Home Ownership Routledge & Kegan Paul, London 1981.

Kemeny, J., 'Home Ownership and Privatization', International Journal of Urban and Regional Research, Vol. 4, 1982, pp. 372-387.

Kilroy, B., Housing Finance - Organic Reform, Labour Economics, Finance and Taxation Association, London 1978.

Lambert, C., Building societies, surveyors and the older areas of Birmingham, Working Paper 38, CURS, University of Birmingham 1976.

Lansley, S. and Goss, S., What Price Housing : a review of housing subsidies and proposals for reforms, SHAC, London 1981.

Liverpool City Council, Housing Strategy Statement, 1979/83, Liverpool City Council, Liverpool 1978.

Liverpool City Council Planning Department, The City's Older Housing Stock : Information Note 1, Liverpool City Planning Department, Liverpool 1981.

McIntosh, N., 'Mortgage Support Scheme Holds the Lending Lines' Roof, Mar-Apr. 1978, pp. 44-47.

Melville Ross, T., 'Down Market Lending by Building Societies', Housing Review, 30, 1981, pp. 126-129.

Merrett, S., Owner Occupation in Britain, Routledge and Kegan Paul, London 1982.

Office of Population Census and Surveys, Census 1981 : County Monitors. HMSO, London 1982.

Paris, C. and Blackaby, B., Not Much Improvement, Heinemann, London 1979.

Robinson, V., 'Asians and Council Housing', Urban Studies, 17, (3) October 1980, pp. 323-332.

Saunders, P., Social Theory and the Urban Question, Hutchinson, London 1981.

Smith, D., The Facts of Racial Disadvantage, Political and Economic Planning, London 1977.

Simmie, J., Power, Property and Corporatism : The Political Sociology of Planning, Macmillan, London 1981.

Stedman, Jones, G., Outcast London, Oxford University Press, London 1971.

Stevens, L., et.al., Race and Building Society Lending in Leeds, Leeds Community Relations Council, Leeds 1982.

US Congress, HUD Investigation of Low and Moderate Income Housing Program, Hearings before the House Committee on Banking and Currency 92nd Congress 1st Sessions; US Government Printing Offices 1971.

Weir, S., 'Red Line Districts', Roof, July 1976, pp. 109-114.

West Midlands County Council, House Condition Survey Preliminary Results, WMCC, Birmingham 1982.

West Midlands County Council, Report of County Planner to Strategic Planning Committee, WMCC, Birmingham 1982.

Wienk, R., et.al., Measuring racial discrimination in American housing markets; the housing market practice survey, Washington DC, 1979.

Wilkinson, R.K. and Gulliver, S., 'The impact of non-whites on house prices' Race, Vol. 13, (1) July 1971, pp. 21-36.

Williams, P., The role of financial institutions in the inner London housing market: the case of Islington, Transactions of the Institute of British Geographers, Vol. 1, 72-81, 1976.

Williams, P., 'Building Societies and the Inner City', Transactions of the Institute of British Geographers. New Series, Vol. 3, 4, 23-24 1978.

Williams, P., 'Restructuring urban managerialism: towards a political economy of urban allocation', Environment and Planning A, 14: 95-105, 1982.

Index